F.A.T.E. 5

Jewel of Jarhen

Jewel of Jarhen

A F.A.T.E. Novel
by
Gregory Kern

MEWS BOOKS
LONDON AND CONNECTICUT

Also by Gregory Kern in this series:

F.A.T.E. 1: Galaxy of the Lost
F.A.T.E. 2: Slave Ship from Sergan
F.A.T.E. 3: Monster of Metaleze
F.A.T.E. 4: Enemy Within the Skull

This work was originally published in the U.S.A. as
CAP KENNEDY No. 5 JEWEL OF JARHEN

Copyright © 1974 by DAW BOOK, INC.
First published in United States of America by Daw Books February 1974

*

FIRST MEWS EDITION SEPTEMBER 1976

*

Mews Books are published by
Mews Books Limited, 20 Bluewater Hill, Westport, Connecticut 06880
and distributed by
New English Library Limited, Barnard's Inn, Holborn, London EC1N 2JR
Made and printed in Great Britain by Hunt Barnard Printing Ltd., Aylesbury, Bucks.

45200038 6

CHAPTER ONE

He woke screaming from a dream in which he had been slowly flayed alive, and stared wild-eyed at the tall figure standing beside his couch.

'My lord.' Nava Sonega moved a little, the light from a lantern touching the engraved hollows of his face. 'You are summoned to attend your brother.'

Umed Khan gulped, reaching for the table on which stood a goblet of wine. It did little to ease his apprehension, but his throat moistened, he was able to speak.

'Why? For what purpose?'

'A hunt, my lord.' Sonega's voice matched his figure, old, sere, the rustle of leaves beneath dormant trees. 'The runes were cast and the omens propitious. Also,' he added dryly, 'a herd of wild drell has been reported from the Frome estate.'

'And my brother is eager to slaughter them.' Umed Khan finished his wine. 'Has he not had enough of killing?'

Nava Sonega made no comment, stepping back as the other rose. The prince was dewed with sweat, in need of a bath and relaxing attention, but there was no time for self-indulgence. Quickly he dressed in boots, breeches, an undershirt of fine metal mesh, a tunic of woven silk ornamented with lizards, the creatures brightly yellow against maroon. A thick cloak and he was ready.

'Arms?'

'Will be provided, my lord. Attendants and nerfs are waiting.' Sonega led the way toward the door, turning as he reached the portal in time to see the other reach for more wine. 'My lord,' he said sharply. 'You have not eaten.'

It was a subtle warning against overindulgence, or as subtle as Umed could expect, but the man was right. Wine was no protection, and the false courage it gave could be dangerous. Now, as always, he would need a clear head if he hoped to survive.

Setting down the decanter, he said, 'I had a dream. I was being slowly flayed and it seemed that my brother watched and enjoyed my pain. Your interpretation?'

'I am not a seer, my lord.'

'And so do not believe in premonitions?' Umed Khan shrugged; over the course of years he had learned to recognize Sonega's caution. 'And yet you must have some guidance to determine your actions. How else could you have survived so long in the court of Jarhen? First with my father, then with my brother, neither noted for their gentle restraint. What charm do you possess which gives you immunity against those who rule?'

'No charm, my lord.' Nava Sonega opened the door. 'No charm, but a little anticipation. The knowledge, for example, that your brother will be irate if kept waiting.'

Umed Khan heard his brother's voice as he descended to the courtyard. A bull-roar heavy with arrogance, it rose to echo from the moldering stone of the palace.

'Fool! My boot! You dare to be so clumsy!'

A man screamed as a whip cracked and Umed saw a groom staggering back from where his brother sat mounted, hands to his eyes, blood running from beneath his fingers. Jarhed laughed thickly, running the lash through a gloved hand.

'He spilled wine on my boot and claimed he had not seen the leather. Well, if I struck true, he will never see again. Now, brother, mount! We have far to go.'

Twenty men accompanied them, riding sullenly through the silence of the predawn city. Slumbering beggars stirred as they passed, waking to cringe at the sight of their lord and his retinue. Only in the great square were there signs of activity; too early for the markets, it was always time for pleasure, and those watching would wait until the end.

They thronged the circle of guards, eyes lifted to stare above and beyond the crested helmets and ceremonial pikes to where, bathed in the light of searchbeams set on surrounding houses, a man was dying.

He was thin, emaciated, ribs stark against the strained parch-

6

ment of his chest. His head was thrown back, the corded throat raw from screaming, the gaping mouth soundless now, able only to mew the pain. Ropes lashed his arms behind his back and supported the bulk of heavy weights lashed to each ankle. Between his thighs the slender cone of polished wood on which he had been impaled was laced with lines of blood, some dried, others glistening wet.

'He's lasted well,' rumbled Jarhed. 'The execution was at sunset. Five will get you ten if he lasts until noon.'

'No,' said Umed.

'Squeamish, brother?' Jarhed's laugh rose above the murmur from the crowd. 'At times I think our father's madness drove him into the arms of a chull and only my mother's charity claimed you for her own.'

Umed felt the hand on his arm, Sonega's quick pressure of warning, and was glad that he had not drunk the second goblet of wine. Instead of the sharp retort against the insult, which would have brought the lash of a whip across his eyes or sent him to follow the dying man on the stake, he said quietly, 'Each to his own, my lord. I gain no pleasure from wagers on dying men.'

Others had no such compunction. From the crowd came the calls of men chanting odds, the comments of those who calculated their chances. Impalement took time to kill. A man could hasten his end by struggling, driving the pointed end deeper into his vitals, bursting intestines, spleen, diaphragm, and lungs, drowning in his own blood. Or he could do the reverse, strive to support his weight by the pressure of his thighs against the polished wood, lengthening his agony by as much as days.

In this case the weights were against the man. With his poor constitution, flabbily muscled and with little reserve, he would barely last until dawn.

Jarhed had wanted a safe gamble.

Umed followed as the big man led the way toward the northern gate, hooves thudding as the column passed from the city and headed into the country beyond. Lights glowed from the spacefield to one side, a patch of brightness against the shimmer of stars, the trail of a comet which laced a skein of brilliance low on the horizon. Higher curtains of luminescence glowed like veils flecked with gems, points of ruby, emerald, sapphire, and agate, murky globes of opal, splinters of diamond,

7

smudges of amber, ebon patches of interstellar dust which shielded the light of suns beyond.

Umed stared at the heavens with interest. Tugool was entering the house of Cran, Armand was in the ascendant, and Tramarg in aspect. All propitious signs. Against them was the fact that Jarhed had summoned him from his bed to join the hunt. He had experienced a troublesome dream, and on retiring, had broken a favorite charm.

His mount stumbled and Umed lowered his head. Signs and omens must be ignored in the need to avoid a fall which could easily break his neck.

At dawn they ate, chewing slabs of dried meat and tough bread as they rode, washing down the rough fare with drafts of bitter wine. An hour before noon their guide halted and pointed with his whip at a clump of vegetation.

'There, my lord,' he said to Jarhed. 'If they have not moved on, the drell should be within.'

'If they are not, you will suffer for it.' Jarhed rose in his stirrups, looking ahead. Beneath him the nerf shifted restlessly, long neck twisting, pointed head staring with lidless eyes back and up at its rider. The tail, docked and tufted with feathers, lashed slowly from side to side. 'Steady, my beauty!' Jarhed's gloved hand slapped at the scaled neck. He was kinder to beasts than to men.

Umed said, 'He could scent the drell, my lord.'

'Can you, brother?' Jarhed's teeth flashed white in the sunlight. 'Is that why you are so pale?'

'Your plans, my lord?' Sonega saved Umed from the necessity of making a reply. 'If the drell are within that copse, I would suggest that we dismount and proceed on foot.'

'So speaks the mighty hunter,' sneered the Lord of Jarhen. 'Any fool knows that a nerf becomes unmanageable at the scent of a drell. Arkon! My gun!'

It was a beautiful weapon, imported from a foreign world, the stock chased with gold in flowing designs. Umed looked enviously at it as he was handed a spear. It was eight feet long, the blade sharply pointed, other blades curving from the shaft three feet from the point. Against an unarmed man it was effective, against a boar ideal, against a drell it was useless.

He said, 'Am I not to have a rifle, my lord?'

'You are of the ruling house, brother. I think it time you displayed your courage. You will stand to my right with

8

Sonega. Arkon, you and Henga to my left. The rest as usual. Beaters, forward!'

Half the men rode forward to the far side of the copse to drive, with yells and shots, anything within to the edge facing them. The rest, aside from those attending the mounts, spread in a wide semicircle behind Jarhed, following as he headed toward the vegetation.

Seven of them, thought Umed. A symbolic number, a lucky one; but for whom?

He glanced from his spear to the rifle Sonega carried. A poor thing compared to Jarhed's, but infinitely better than any spear. Arkon, too, carried a rifle; Henga a spear. The pattern, at least, was symmetrical, but that brought little comfort. Henga too could be a sacrifice. Despite the sun Umed felt a sudden chill.

Had he been summoned to the hunt so as to die the victim of a contrived accident?

Portents had not been lacking. At a farm near Comarch a kraked had been born with three heads, at another close to Lapah a flight of birds had wheeled to form strange patterns in the sky before descending to peck a bull-nerf to death. Red snow had been seen in the desert, and a volcano, long quiescent, had fumed into noxious life. A comet flamed in the sky, and in the city, a prophet had foretold of dire events.

Harbingers of fate, thought Umed Khan sickly. He had carelessly ignored the signs pointing to the future. And his recent dream – he should have pleaded sickness, fallen from his mount, anything. But now it was too late.

'My lord,' whispered Sonega. 'If anything should come our way, allow me to fire. Remain behind and to one side. If I should fall – run.'

'You think me a coward, Nava?'

'Better a live coward than a dead hero,' said the old man bluntly. 'That spear is useless. Flight may not save you from a charging drell, but to attack it with that is to commit suicide.' He added softly, 'And do not forget, my lord, you are next in line to the throne.'

That was reason enough for Jarhed to want him dead. Cabals could be formed, rebellions fostered, but without a focal point they would be that much less dangerous. Umed swallowed and felt his palms grow slippery with sweat. He wiped them, gripped the shaft of the useless spear, lowered the point toward the shielding vegetation.

Something scuttled from under a bush and he felt his heart leap. Jarhed fired, and a tiny body lifted beneath the impact of the bullet, fur and bone and blood smashed into an unrecognizable pulp. Above the rolling echoes of the shot came the voices of the beaters, the sharp sounds they made, and something more. A hiss like that of escaping air. A rumble. The sound of snapping twigs and breaking roots. The roar of a drell.

It burst around them like a clap of thunder, quivering the air with raw power, the blast sending leaves falling from arching branches. It came again, a third time, then the brush parted and nightmare rushed forward.

It was huge, an old bull, the scaled hide warted and scarred from ancient combats. The head was two-thirds jaw, parted to show gleaming fangs, the red of tongue and throat throwing the razor incisors into sharp prominence. The snout was horned, the axillary appendages to either side of the head reaching forward, claws like hooks to snare and drag prey to the gaping maw. The legs were like the boles of trees, the hooves pads of crushing destruction. And it was fast.

Umed had only a glimpse of the creature, then he felt the impact of air against his face, the thick, harsh stench clogging his nostrils and stinging his eyes. Through tears he saw the beast suddenly lurch in front of him, and he dropped, lifting the spear in a futile gesture. Sonega fired, a thread of flame sending lead smashing against the scaled armor, bullets whining in ricochet. He was aiming for an eye, thought Umed, hoping to blast the sight from one of the orbs buried deep in protective bone. He missed, but came close enough to veer the creature from its path. It slewed a little and thundered to where Jarhed stood.

The Lord of Jarhen stood his ground, the rifle hard against his cheek, finger tensed to send blasting missiles into the throat, the spine, the brain of the drell. He had time to take careful aim, confident that the weapon he carried was equal to the task, and he closed his finger.

And lost his smile as nothing happened.

He closed his finger again, heard the dry click, and lowered the rifle to tear at the bolt. Too late, he recognized his danger. He stood for a moment, numb, then turned and tried to run.

The drell caught him at the third step. The head lowered, lifted, the horn impaling a struggling shape, jerking to throw it clear, passing over it and leaving a red smear where a head had

10

been. Umed watched, shocked by the speed of events, unable to move, to shout a command. And then, as if stung to life, the attendants moved in, guns firing, their roar drowning that of the drell, bullets smashing into the great bulk to bring it down to its knees, to its side. It rolled to rest, lifeless jaws gaping toward the empty sky.

Umed looked at it, then at the thing it had left crushed into the ground. The headless, impaled creature lying in a pool of blood and intestines, less now than the dirt on which it lay. His brother, the Lord of Jarhen. Abruptly he was very sick.

'My lord!' Nava Sonega stood over him, a goblet of wine in his hand. 'Drink this, my lord.'

Umed sipped at the wine. It held a sharp tang as if of herbs. Cautiously he handed back the goblet.

'A stimulant, my lord,' said the old man easily. 'You have suffered a shock. Your brother – ' He glanced at the mess on the ground.

'It could have been me,' muttered Umed. 'If you hadn't veered, the beast – '

'We could both have died.' Deliberately Sonega took a swallow of the wine, a silent reassurance that it contained nothing harmful. 'But we did not. Fate guarded us both.'

'But not my brother.' Umed frowned. 'He was going to fire. I saw his finger press the trigger. Twice. He would have killed the beast.'

'It could be that he missed.'

'No.' Jarhed had been a superb shot. 'He did not miss. The rifle did not fire.'

He saw the veil fall over Sonega's eyes, and became aware of the abrupt silence which fell all around. In it, remarkably clear, the voices of the beaters echoed through the copse. The voices, nothing more, and that was strange. A herd of wild drell had been reported and there should have been cows and even cubs, but there had been nothing aside from the one old bull. One bull and a rifle which had malfunctioned. Had he read the portents aright?

Arkon dragged one boot over the ground. 'My lord, shall we call off the hunt?'

Umed nodded, thinking, remembering the delay before the attendants had fired, the way in which Sonega had turned the charge of the beast. Would Arkon have done the same had it headed in his direction? Could he have done anything else?

11

Jarhed had always insisted on the right to kill. To rob him of that pleasure would be to invite the stake. And yet . . .

He walked to where the rifle had fallen. A hoof had twisted the barrel, smearing the gold in the stock, but the bolt still worked and Umed operated it, staring at the cartridge which had rested in the chamber. The primer bore the clear mark of the pin. A misfire, then. He had proof that the gun had worked.

'Fate,' whispered Sonega at his side. Unheard, the man had joined him. A cartridge which did not fire. Who could have prevented it?'

Had Jarhed lived he would have found an answer. The armorer for one, his assistant, the importer of the ammunition, the beaters even, certainly the attendants who had taken so long to fire. All would have screamed out their lives on the stake. They could still do it. With a start, Umed realized that he was now Lord of Jarhen.

'One shot,' he said slowly. 'It would take more than luck for one shot to kill a drell.'

'True, my lord.'

'And yet it could have happened. If Jarhed hadn't fired at the small creature, he could be alive now.'

'Even so, my lord. But what man can avoid his fate.'

No one, and if the cartridge had been tampered with, did it make that much difference? Jarhed could have fired again before the drell had charged. He could have been quicker to work the bolt. He could have run or not come on the hunt at all. A thousand things could have saved him if fate had not sealed the moment of his death.

'Your brother is dead, my lord,' said Sonega flatly. 'And now you rule Jarhen. No longer need you fear dreams and portents of evil . . . And omens are not always what they seem.'

He was right, of course. Radiation could induce a mutation, and birds at times behaved in illogical ways. Red snow was not new, and shiftings of the planetary crust had wakened volcanoes before. Comets were normal, and the prophet could be deranged or delirious. Yet, in a universe composed mostly of the unknown, any guide was better than none.

And, thought Umed cynically, it was not always wise to look a gift horse in the mouth.

Dropping the cartridge to the ground, he drove it into the soil with the heel of his boot. 'An accident,' he said. 'A thing impossible to have prevented. And who am I to argue against the dictates of fate? The custody of Jarhen has been given to me.'

He heard Sonega's indrawn breath, the sigh of what could have been relief. It traveled on invisible wings so that Arkon relaxed, as did the others, voices softly breaking the silence that had hung over them like a cloud.

Sonega said, 'And now, my lord?'

'We return to the city?'

'And?'

Umed smiled, straightening, throwing back his shoulders and breathing deep of the scented air. 'You mock at portents, Nava, but they are very real. And all men, whether they know it or not, admit it or not, are but instruments of fate. You are such a one, I another. We exist only as parts of a master plan. Would it surprise you to learn that, when I was very young, a seer foretold what would happen today?'

'No, my lord.' Sonega was impatient. 'But the young are easily impressed and hindsight a simple exercise. As the younger brother by a year any accident could have lifted you to the throne. And I venture to suggest that the seer you speak of did not give details.'

'No,' admitted Umed. 'He did not. But the facts suffice. Now I rule.'

'To hunt, to kill, to pleasure yourself regardless of the welfare of Jarhen?' Sonega was too bold. 'As your father did before, killing himself with the misuse of exotic drugs? As your brother did before – ' He broke off, glancing to where men lifted a bound shape to the back of a nerf. 'You will forgive me if I speak bluntly, my lord, but I would be a poor adviser if I did not. Jarhed cannot continue alone. We need help and resources we cannot afford. To insist on complete independence is to face inevitable financial ruin and total domination by an aggressive power. This has been obvious for many years. However, your father – '

'Played at the despot and indulged his every whim.'

' – refused to consider the matter.' Sonega ignored the interruption. 'And your brother – '

'Played the same game for a dozen years.'

' – also insisted on following his own desires. Now we can afford to wait no longer. Representations have been made and it is time to decide which path Jarhen will follow.'

'To whom we will give our allegiance, you mean.'

13

'Not so, my lord. To determine with whom we shall form an alliance. There is a difference, as I am sure you appreciate. As you will appreciate that a decision has to be made and our future decided.'

Umed climbed into the saddle and looked down at Sonega's face. 'You had better mount,' he said. 'We have far to travel.'

'My lord?'

'And it would be best not to travel too quickly in case we should fall.'

CHAPTER TWO

All was quiet in the *Mordain*. With the ship on automatic control, clear space ahead and nothing urgently demanding attention, it was time to relax. In the compact laboratory Kennedy picked up a knife.

It was double-edged, the blade ten inches long, razor-sharp and needle-pointed, the haft whorled so as to provide a snug grip. He spun it, caught it by the point, lifted his arm and with a smooth coordination of effort threw it at the snarling face of a man. Light splintered from the blade as it lanced through the air. Inches from the staring eyes it jerked sideways to thud into the wood surrounding the target.

'That's five times in succession, Jarl,' he said. 'It looks as if you're on the right track.'

Professor Jarl Luden shook his head and pursed his thin lips as if he had tasted something sour.

'As yet I have made little progress, Cap. The hysteresis effect has been known for centuries, and although I have made some improvement, it still leaves much to be desired. The problem is one of velocity. The faster a missile cuts the lines of force the greater is the energy generated within and the more complete the destruction. With a slow-moving object such as a thrown knife the relative energy levels are too small. I have managed to deflect it, but the equipment necessary is too clumsy for personal use.'

'I warned you that the simple reduction of the normal meteor protective field wouldn't work.'

'You did,' snapped Luden. 'And I had no intention of miniaturizing standard ship equipment. In order to deal with low-velocity missiles a new approach was necessary. You have seen the result – failure.'

Kennedy raised his eyebrows. Without comment he retrieved the knife, and moving to the far end of the laboratory, threw it again at the target.

'Failure,' repeated Luden as it thudded into the wood. 'Had you stabbed instead of thrown, the blade would have gone home. I must try a new approach bearing in mind the essential elements desired in the construct. A personal body-shield must be inconspicuous, automatically activated, able to prevent the impact of any missile coming from any direction at any velocity, be capable of handling objects of varying composition individually and in groups, and protect the wearer from radiation and extremes of temperature.'

'For optimum performance, yes,' agreed Kennedy. 'But I'd be willing to settle for something which would give protection against solid missiles. It would be better than what we have now.'

'Allow me to correct you,' snapped Luden precisely. 'We already have such protection. We call it armor. The difference would only be in weight and convenience. Well, I had better dismantle this toy.'

Kennedy leaned back against the edge of the wide desk as he watched the other at work. Luden offered a direct contrast to his own tall, well-proportioned figure neat in black and gold. The professor was grave, his sparse form dressed in gaudy fabrics. Thick gray hair was swept back from a high forehead. His eyes were blue, deep-set, and alight with intelligence; he was a man who had spent his life in the pursuit of knowledge.

He said, 'This is irritating, Cap. We know from logic and legend that personal body-shields must have been known to other races. The Zheltyana, certainly, must have used them. Any race able to expand through the galaxy would have possessed the science necessary for their construction, and we know that they touched on many worlds, some unsuited for life as we know it. Either they were incredibly adaptive or used some means to control their environment; if so, personal protection would have been of major importance.'

'An assumption we have no right to make, Jarl. We don't know enough about them.'

No one did. Only the fact that they had once existed could

16

not be denied. A race of beings, incredibly ancient, which had flowered to spread throughout the known galaxy and leave enigmatic traces on a host of worlds. They had left a sign of convoluted, interwound circles, and mysterious artifacts and fragments the purpose of which was unknown. As was the fate which had caused them to vanish.

'We have clues,' Luden reminded him. 'Legends are full of hints. Shields, belts, rings, helmets which gave their wearer invulnerability.'

'Magic.'

'Magic,' agreed Luden. 'Or science. In primitive cultures the terms are interchangeable, and a man can only describe what he sees in terms of what he knows. Gods descending from the skies wearing items of mysterious power. Young races using the discarded remnants of the Zheltyana, perhaps, Trading expeditions which left nothing but distorted memories. Well, one day perhaps, we shall know.'

It was a dream that they both held; Kennedy for as long as he could remember. To solve the secret of the ancient race, their origins and their end. He glanced at the racked files in the laboratory, items culled from a thousand worlds, indexed and correlated with painstaking care.

He said thoughtfully, 'A belt of power – that would be a field generator, but need the field be exactly as we know it? A time-distortion effect would serve to give invulnerability. If a bullet, for example, could be thrown back or forward in time? Forward by a little would cause it to miss. Or it could be thrown out of phase – '

'Vibratory realignment?' Luden nodded, thoughtful. 'It could be the answer, Cap. There would have to be a nullifying field to protect the wearer – ' He broke off as a yell echoed through the vessel. 'What the devil is that?'

It was Penza Saratov. His voice rose again as Kennedy entered the engine room.

'Veem! You damned freak! I'll paste you on the bulkhead for this!'

Relaxation, to Penza, was exercise. He had rigged up a complicated arrangement of springs and levers in which now he appeared to be hopelessly snared, arms and legs intermeshed with links and couplings, the shaven ball of his head rising like a melon from constricting bars.

Looking at him, Kennedy was reminded of a troglodyte from

2

Earth's ancient mythology. A creature almost as wide as he was tall, his head running into massive shoulders, a barrel chest matching the thickness of his limbs. A living machine of flesh, bone, and muscle. A giant born and raised of a world with three times the normal gravity of Earth.

Dressed in his normal loose garments, he appeared to be a normal man grown impossibly obese, but he was far from being a soft mass of useless blubber. The vast frame carried not an ounce of useless fat; all was sinew and toughness, trained and controlled strength. As a ship engineer he was the finest Kennedy had ever met.

He said, 'Cap, can you see him?'

'Who?'

'That freak, of course. Veem did this and now he's watching from somewhere laughing his fool head off. I'll make him laugh!'

Smiling, Kennedy said, 'What happened?'

'I was exercising. A man has to keep in condition. I'd set the machine for four gravities and then something broke. That freak weakened a coupling and released the springs.' Penza tensed and metal grated as he pulled himself free. 'When I find him I'll teach him a lesson. A coat of paint will teach him not to be so clever in the future.'

His anger was more simulated than real, but he had reason to be annoyed. Stepping forward, Kennedy examined the machine. One of the links had yielded, metal bright at the break.

'Veem wasn't responsible for this, Penza. You overloaded the tension and forgot the harmonics. Constant use has caused metal fatigue.'

Saratov blinked. 'You're sure, Cap?'

'Check it with the electronscope if you like, but I know what you'll find. There's no trace of acid or mechanical interference.' He added, 'Maybe you owe Veem an apology.'

'Apologize to that freak?' Saratov inflated his chest. 'So I was wrong,' he admitted, 'but if I apologize to him, I'll never hear the last of it. I'll make him a cup of coffee instead.' He glowered around the engine room. 'That's if I can find him. If not, he'll have to go without.'

Veem Chemile was in the kitchen. He stood before the ultrawave oven and rested his hand on the chronometer. As he concentrated the hand appeared to vanish, to merge with the surface and display the dial which it covered. He concentrated

18

even more and the hand appeared, moving, counting seconds. As Saratov appeared, he froze.

The giant didn't see him. Muttering, he drew water to fill the percolator, then stood rubbing at the welts caused by the impact of the springs.

Chemile said hollowly, 'Beware, Penza, your sins will find you out.'

'Veem!' Saratov spun, eyes searching the small compartment. 'Where the hell are you?'

He grunted as the oven seemed to dissolve, to take the shape of a man. Veem Chemile was tall, thin, with a sweep of hair over sloping brows and eyes which looked like tiny points in the smooth ovoid of his face. His ears were small and set tight against his skull. He moved with a fluid grace on soundless feet, to stand grinning at the discomforted giant.

'I heard,' he said. 'That coffee had better be good, Penza. I don't want any of your usual swill.'

'You'll get what you're given,' snapped the giant. 'If you weren't always hiding, eavesdropping, and listening to private conversations, you wouldn't get blamed for what you hadn't done. What are you up to, anyway?'

'Practicing.' Chemile rested his hand over the chronometer. 'See? I can even make the hand appear and move as you'd expect. That takes talent. When you came in I just froze.'

In a strange, half alive condition in which his metabolism slowed, his skin, scaled with minute flecks of photosensitive tissue, adopted the coloration of the background against which he stood. He was a man-sized chameleon with an infinitely superior protective mechanism, developed on the harsh world which had given him birth.

Saratov said, 'You should take more physical exercise. That's the trouble with these journeys, no chance to get a really good workout. A man gets rusty unless he keeps in trim.'

'I manage.'

'And what good does it do you? I could snap you in two without raising a sweat. Tricks are all very well, but a man has to have strength at times. Real strength. Coat you with paint and you'd be useless.' Saratov poured coffee and handed Chemile a cup. 'Here. If you don't like it, that's just too bad.'

'Taking some to the others?'

'Of course.'

'I shouldn't.' Chemile sipped and shook his head. 'You're

19

good at some things, Penza, but making coffee isn't one of them. Tell you what; why don't you just use this sludge to clean the engines and I'll make you a real brew.'

The chime of the communicator drowned Saratov's reply.

Director Elias Weyburn carried the weight of worlds on his shoulders, and at times it showed. He looked from the screen, his face drawn, beaked nose giving him the appearance of a brooding eagle. Without ceremony he said, 'Cap, you're needed.'

Kennedy was equally curt. 'Where?'

'Jarhen. It's a world at the edge of the Inchonian Enclave – I'll send the coordinates and basic data. There's been a power shift and the world is ripe for assimilation. Normally Terran Control wouldn't be interested, but MALACA Eight has reported the discovery of rare metals on an asteroid of the Phugian System. In order to maintain direct lines of communication Jarhen needs to be incorporated into the Terran Sphere.'

'So?'

'There are complications. The Inchonians want it and so do the Chambodians. We can guess why. Those damned vultures want to spread their wings too far and it would suit them to move in and take over.'

Kennedy said, 'What do the Jarhenians feel about it?'

'Nothing; they aren't being consulted. The prime factor is Umed Khan. He took the throne when his brother got himself killed. This is strictly a one-man affair. The world operates on a feudal basis, and I doubt if they've ever heard of elections or the democratic process. It's raw, rough, and primitive, but it happens to be in just the right section of space to be important. We want it because of the new discoveries. Inchon wants it because it offers a close market and labor supply. Chambodia wants it to gain a forward base and to score against Terra. We know how they feel about us and it's mutual.'

Kennedy frowned, wondering how he came into it. On the face of it, the matter was simple. Terra would send a delegation, make the best offer, and Jarhen would become a unit of the Terran Sphere. Once incorporated, they could ask for the assistance of a Mobile Aid Laboratory and Construction Authority to help raise their standard of living and to provide protection against any outside aggression. A simple matter of bargaining without need for secret agents.

Weyburn said, 'You're wondering how this affects you, Cap. Right?'

'I assume there are complications.'

'Aren't there always?' Weyburn sounded bitter. 'In this case it's something special. To put it bluntly, by all normal standards Umed Khan is a nut. He's sold on mysticism, omens, all that stuff. Before he would agree to negotiate he had to wait for an auspicious occasion determined by seers, astrologers, and assorted practitioners of the arcane arts. Well, we went along. The thing is that our delegate is no longer able to function. We have a time limit and you are the only one close enough to beat it. As a Free Acting Terran Envoy you have full authority to negotiate on behalf of Terran Control.'

'Openly?'

'It's unusual, Cap, but yes, openly. Not as a member of FATE, of course, but as our accredited delegate. Come to think of it, you're the best one we could send.'

Kennedy doubted it. He was a man of action and had small liking for diplomatic maneuvering. That took a special type of mind belonging to a man who loved to wage war with words and who could sense a lie from the truth by the lift of an eyebrow. Only when everything else had failed and the *Pax Terra* was at stake did Weyburn send for him to cut the Gordian Knot.

Like all Free Acting Terran Envoys Kennedy usually worked in the dark, carrying supreme authority, acting as judge, jury, and executioner, assassin too if the need arose and madness threatened the peace of innocent worlds. He did the work that had to be done without recognition, satisfied with successful results.

'I mean it,' said Weyburn. 'You've had experience, the Metelaze affair, and that time on Doong. And we're up against something odd.'

'Sorcery?'

'Maybe. Dirty work, anyway.'

'Your delegate,' said Kennedy, remembering. 'You said he had ceased to function. Hurt?'

'Dead,' Weyburn was curt. 'He was found in his room drowned to death.'

'Drowned?'

'His lungs were full of brine.' Weyburn gave a baffled gesture. 'Don't ask me how it was done – I don't know. His aide, Stuart Seward, found him. He had obviously retired and settled down for the night. The covers were dry and so was his night attire,

21

but he had drowned. Seward held the body in freeze and sent it to Commander Mbomoma of MALACA Eight. You can get a full report from him. Activate your copier and stand by for transmitted data. Scramset two-three-seven-one.'

Kennedy adjusted the control. A green lamp flashed and a sheaf of papers dropped from the slot beneath the screen.

'You've got three days to get there, Cap,' ended Weyburn. 'The *Mordain*'s the only ship that could do it. Luck.'

They were already on their way. Luden had caught the papers and given the coordinates to Chemile, who now sat at the controls, altering course and feeding full power to the drive. Saratov, beaming at the prospect of action, dismantled his apparatus, listening intently for any jarring note from the coils of his perfectly tuned engines. Luden, precise as always, studied the papers with a thoughtful expression.

'I can understand what Weyburn meant when he mentioned Metelaze, Cap, but there is no true parallel. There we had to deal with a deliberately introduced cult designed for a specific purpose, but as far as I can discern, Jarhen is a world genuinely steeped in primitive superstition. Such a culture is not new, of course. Back in early times primitive societies leaned heavily on omens and oracles. Babylon, Persia, even Rome, despite a high level of civilization. The Egyptians based their practice of medicine on magic and religious incantations, and all early societies used amulets and charms. Astrology, palmistry, necromancy, augury, the casting of runes were all attempts to decipher the unknown and to gain guidance for future action. The interesting thing is that, even beneath the impact of modern technology, such beliefs could exist in an official capacity.'

'I'm more interested in what happened to our delegate,' said Kennedy. 'A man doesn't drown while lying in bed.'

Commander Mbomoma was a big man, muscular shoulders straining at the blue, green, and silver of his uniform, his skin a glistening ebon on the screen, his grizzled hair close-cropped to his skull. His eyes were a liquid jet, the corners creased with a mesh of tiny lines.

'Cap!' He smiled, teeth starkly white against the redness of his mouth. 'It's good to see you again. How have you been?'

'Busy.'

'And not just nurse-maiding empty space, I'll bet. Some people have all the luck. Got anything for me?'

'A question. How does a man drown while lying in bed?'

'He doesn't,' said Mbomoma immediately. 'But I know what you're getting at. It shouldn't have happened, but it did. I've had my medics take the body apart for complete examination, and there's no doubt as to how Ben Hiton died. His lungs were full of salt water and it was genuine brine. Even the mineral trace elements were present. His stomach was full too, just what you'd expect from a drowned man. Apparently that's just what happened.'

'Drowned? In bed?'

The commander shrugged. 'Don't ask me how it could happen. I'm just the office boy around here.'

Kennedy smiled at the understatement, guessing at its cause. Like all MALACA commanders Mbomoma was a victim of his own frustration. Controlling power enough to destroy worlds, he had to exercise constant restraint in the face of provocation. A military diplomat, he walked a razor's edge, burdened with the knowledge that he and those like him were the only visible safeguard of the worlds united in the Terran Sphere.

'You'd like to move in and slap a few wrists,' said Kennedy. 'Teach whoever is responsible for Hiton's death that it doesn't pay to mess around with our people. Right?'

'You said it, Cap. I didn't.'

'If you didn't feel that way, you wouldn't be human, Commander. Did your people find anything unusual? A drug, for example? Something which would have caused fluid to fill his lungs and stomach?'

'No.'

'Any damage to the oral membranes?'

'You're thinking that perhaps someone shoved a funnel down his mouth and poured the brine in,' said Mbomoma. 'I thought of that too. Forget it. There is no trace of damage.'

'Then what's your opinion?'

'Magic,' said the commander promptly. 'When all reasonable explanations don't apply, that's all there is left. Someone hexed him. From what I know about Jarhen that is more than possible.'

Kennedy said patiently, 'One day you'll have to argue the point with the professor. Jarl would love to have you demonstrate just what a hex is and how it works. Any unusual activity in the area of space surrounding Jarhen?'

'More ships have been landing than usual. I can't put units

23

into the area, of course, but I've kept a scan operating. No great concentration as yet, but it could happen. You want me to move in?'

'Not yet.' Mbomoma, thought Kennedy, was a little too eager. 'We don't want to trigger an incident. Just have a few units handy in case of need. In the meantime, keep up your scan.' He added, 'How's your boy getting on?'

The teeth were dazzling as the commander smiled. 'Fine, Cap. He's passed three grades and no sign of slowing down. Give him a few years and he'll be where you are now. A Free Acting Terran Envoy! The top!'

'I'll watch for him,' promised Kennedy. 'If he's like his dad, he'll be treading on my heels.'

Luden said as he turned from the screen, 'I don't think Mbomoma was joking, Cap. About the hex, I mean. It is barely possible that the delegate could have been killed by hypnotic suggestion. That, after all, is the motivating power behind what is termed a hex. Persuade the victim that you have power over him and he will respond to any threat you care to make. The Australian aborigines, for example, had the power of dealing death by pointing a bone. It requires only a little imagination to draw an analogy between a bone and a gun. Both are pointed. In one case knowledge takes the place of a bullet; the knowledge that the action alone is sufficient to kill.'

'Providing the victim believes it,' said Kennedy. 'Ben Hiton was the product of a modern civilization. He knew better than to believe in such things.'

'But he is dead.'

'A man can die in many ways.'

'True.' Luden riffled the sheets he had been studying. 'You know, Cap, I feel that this is going to be a most interesting assignment.'

CHAPTER THREE

They landed at night, the *Mordain* settling between the scarred hull of a freighter and the sleek lines of a vessel designed for war. Drums stirred the air, the sound carried from the city by a cool breeze from the ocean, the sonorous rhythm like the beat of a monstrous heart. A young man was waiting.

'Captain Kennedy, sir?' He held out his hand. 'I am Stuart Seward. I was told to expect you. I am glad you could make it in time.'

Kennedy took the proffered hand. The fingers were slender, the grip firm and cool. The aide was tall, neat in his diplomatic uniform, his eyes deep-set, steady. Not a man to jump to wild conclusions and one trained to mask his emotions. He showed no sign of the relief he must have felt at their arrival.

Kennedy said, 'How long have we got?'

'Until Tugool reaches the zenith. That's about an hour before dawn. A hell of a time to start a conference, but apparently all the signs point to it as being auspicious to the destiny of Jarhen.' He hesitated. 'I'm afraid that doesn't leave much time for me to fill you in on the background.'

'That won't be necessary, young man,' said Luden acidly. 'We have had plenty of time to do our homework. I suggest that you guide us at once to our quarters. I assume rooms have been placed at our disposal in the palace?'

'A suite in the east wing.' Stuart glanced at Kennedy. 'Your ship?'

'It's safe.' Locked, the *Mordain* would require a wrecking crew to gain unauthorized entry. Smiling, Kennedy added,

'Don't let the professor throw you – any help you can give will be welcome.' He tilted his head, listening to the drums. 'A celebration?'

'The festival of the spring equinox. Everyone goes a little wild. They – well, you'll be able to see for yourself.'

He led the way from the field, Kennedy at his side, Luden a little behind, the rear taken up with Saratov and Chemile. The giant wore his usual loose robes and looked more like a fat merchant than the hardened veteran of space he was. Chemile wore a hooded robe adorned with mystic symbols, a garment, he had insisted, which would give him both protection and respect from a superstition-riddled culture.

The gate was open, the drawbridge lowered, guards wearing plated armor and bearing long pikes were standing to either side. The wind caught the flames of flambeaux set in iron sockets on the high walls, painting the scene with ruby light, the flames seeming to rise and die to the beat of the drums so that shadows ran, reaching, to shrink in sudden pools of darkness.

Beyond the gate lay bedlam.

Above the pulse of the drums rose a medley of voices, screams, shouts, chanted incantations, the snarl of quarrels, the soft purr of invitation.

'My lords! Read your fate in the blood of a virgin. A volunteer from Lamach willing to yield her life for the good of all. Ten zesh will gain you a place in the circle . . .'

'The mystic runes of Cromek cast by an adept of the Hillia school. Five zesh will give you the hour of your death, the moment of supreme joy. Will your wife bear a son? Your daughter wed riches? The runes will tell . . .'

'Your fate is graven in the lines of your palm. Read what awaits and avoid misfortune. The true blood of ten generations of seers at your disposal for a single coin. Come, shed all fear, see what the future holds . . .'

Chemile slowed to be jerked forward by a snatch of a big hand.

'No time for that,' snapped Saratov. 'Keep an eye on the others.'

He strode forward as the aide halted, pressing the bulk of his body protectively behind the slight figure of Luden. Before Seward a girl spun, charms tinkling around her throat, short skirt lifting to show the smooth columns of her thighs. Her breasts were bare, painted, and whorls of color spiraled over her torso. Sweat gleamed on the satin flesh. In her right hand was a knife, her left arm was smeared with blood from a multitude of tiny cuts. From her gaping mouth spouted gibberish.

'A chull,' explained Seward. 'Mad, depraved, running wild. She'll dance and cut until she falls unconscious from exhaustion or loss of blood.'

Luden was interested. 'In expiation?'

Seward's tone held respect. 'You know?'

'I told you that we had done our homework. However, I am not sure as to her exact reason for acting as she does. Scapegoats are common in most primitive societies, but usually the punishment is not self-inflicted. In this case I assume the girl is of low moral caliber, and under the influence of hysteria, is seeking to cleanse herself of sin.' He shook his head as the girl spun away, leaving a trail of blood behind her. 'It is truly amazing how strong can be the desire to purge a sense of guilt.'

'It isn't quite that,' said Seward. 'The element of sacrifice is present also, and an appeal to fate for future rewards.'

He pressed on. A narrow street was filled with a dancing column of men and women, each with hands to the hips of the one before, feet moving in time to the drums. As they passed, a man cried out and spun, knife flashing, one hand to his throat.

'My charm! Someone has stolen my charm!'

A beggar whined, lifting blank eyes to the lanterns which he could not see.

'Give of your charity, lords. Good fortune attends the charitable. Aid your fate by being generous.'

A woman whispered, 'Soft flesh, my lords. Young girls trained in ancient skills. My house is filled with pleasures.'

Kennedy watched it all, listening, evaluating. The air held more than the pulse of drums; there was the rank scent of naked hysteria, the reek of superstitious fear. The shouts and screams were ungovernable releases of tension, the stalls and booths busy, not with idle pleasure seekers, but with those desperate to know what the future would bring.

Well, he thought, soon it would change. Traders and strangers would bring other ideas, news of cultures in which merchants did not consult astrologers before closing a deal, farmers did not slit the stomachs of animals in order to determine which crops should be planted and when. Travelers would come from worlds where lucky charms were worn for adornment, if at all, and not handed down from generation to generation as indispensable items of successful living; where men, blindly perhaps, made their own destinies and did not rely on portents and omens.

They reached the great square, cluttered now with stalls, merchants selling lengths of fabrics, rings, beads, chains of hammered brass, constructs of finely blown glass and filigree. A leather-lunged man chanted the virtue of his wares, knives which would stay eternally sharp if held in sheaths of charmed material, belts which would give immunity from plague, boils, and disease. Another, feathered like a bird, sold an unguent which would enable a man to fly if he wore it while chanting the correct incantation.

Luden said dryly, 'You know, Cap, some things are universal. Always there are those eager to seize an opportunity, and the more superstitious a world is, the easier their task.'

'That's true,' admitted Kennedy. Glancing behind, he said, 'Where the devil is Penza?'

The giant was busy at a stall. His big hands held a delicate fabrication of wire and crystal, an ornament designed to be worn around a woman's throat. The vendor was effusive.

'A genuine artifact from ancient times, my lord. I make no idle claim when I say that it is unique. Worn by the woman of your choice, it will make her blind to the appeal of others. Give it to a queen and you will be her king. And there is more.' His voice lowered to a conspiring whisper. 'This can open the door of what-is-to-come. Bathed in the blood of a virgin culled at the juxtaposition of Tugool and Arogel, held in the light of a torch made of harah wood dusted with lamilite voices will murmur of events yet to be. If I were not a poor man a thousand zesh would not win it from my hand. As it is a hundred will make it yours.'

Saratov grunted. 'Five.'

'You mock, my lord. Or perhaps I misheard. Fifty, you said?'

Saratov grunted again. 'Ten.'

The vendor howled as if bitten by a dog, raising his hands to the blue-white glow of the lantern above, his voice plaintive as he launched into a new description of his goods. The howl was artifice, the dissertation a preliminary to more bargaining. Kennedy cut it short.

'You want it, Penza?'

'Yes, Cap, but not at his price.'

'Why?'

28

Saratov lowered his voice. 'Look at it, Cap. Those stones are a dexter form of lamilite and piezoelectric. Those wires are set within the stones, see?' He turned the artifact. 'It's my guess this isn't what it seems. I could be wrong, but if this isn't a crude form of communication device I'll eat it.'

He was probably wrong, but it was worth paying to find out. Kennedy called to Seward: 'Have you money? Good. Give me thirty zesh.' He threw the coins before the vendor. 'Satisfied? Come on, Penza.'

The giant hesitated. 'Where's Veem?'

Chemile had wandered off into the crowd. Kennedy caught a glimpse of a tall, cowled shape and thrust himself toward it. Beneath the light of a blood-red lantern an emaciated man sat before a small table. Behind him stood cages of small animals like rats, and a young boy stood immobile before them. On the table, lying in a pool of blood, rested the disemboweled body of one of the creatures.

'An augur.' Seward sounded his disgust. 'For a price he will read your future in the intestines of a beast.'

'You deride the ancient science?' The old man had sharp ears. Lifting his head, he stared directly at the little group. 'Strangers,' he said. 'What can you know of secret arts? Does the veil of what-is-to-be open at your command?'

'It does,' said Chemile.

'A master?' The old seer frowned at the ornamented robe.

'An adept.' Chemile's voice deepened, became a hollow boom. 'In sand I have read the fate of worlds. In the liquid from secret fruits I have seen the destiny of stars. In the configurations of planets I have discerned the shape of events to come. I – '

He broke off as Saratov gripped his arm. 'Veem,' snapped the giant. 'Quit acting the fool.'

From the crowd a man said, 'Does he jest? Does he mock our beliefs?'

The voice was dangerous. In such an atmosphere it would require little to trigger the release of accumulated violence. Quickly Kennedy said, 'He does not mock. In humility he comes to learn.'

'To learn? An adept?'

'From a distant world,' said Kennedy. 'One on which the skills of the seers of Jarhen are reputed to be great.'

'And Shemarh is the greatest,' called a man. 'At the last festival he read my fate and every detail came true. If the adept wants to learn, he has come to the source of wisdom.'

Other voices echoed him, the crowd pressing near to hem the little group close to the table. Seward whispered, 'We had better make a break for it, sir. The palace isn't far and there will be guards to offer protection.'

Kennedy shook his head. The crowd was too close, and if they tried to run for it, knives would appear and be used. There was a better way. Before he could speak the aged seer said, 'Ten zesh, my lord. That is my fee.'

'Pay him,' said Kennedy. As Seward dropped coins on the table Chemile extended his hand. The old man ignored it.

To Kennedy he said, 'Point to any animal you choose. That one? Good. Now take it in your hands.'

It was small, warm, nibbling at his fingers with sharp teeth. Kennedy restrained the impulse to let it go. Around him the crowd waited, pressing forward; to deny them their entertainment would be to beg for trouble. He heard Chemile's whisper followed by Saratov's deep rumble.

'Cap! You can't – '

'Shut up, Veem! You got us into this.'

Luden said, 'This is most interesting and, in a sense, an acute test of his powers. Prophecies, by their very nature, tend to be unsatisfyingly vague. I expect no more than casual and undefinitive generalizations, but even so it will be an experience.'

Shemarh said, 'Place the beast on the table.'

The boy had cleared away the previous remains and wiped the surface clean. As Kennedy set down the creature the seer held it with strong fingers and picked up a knife with his free hand. It was quickly and expertly done, the animal could have felt no pain, the slash which had opened the body from neck to tail had brought instant death.

In the silence all could hear the sharp intake of the augur's breath.

'You come from afar,' he said. 'From a place which has never known the light of our sun. Among your people you are a person of great power and responsibility. Now you carry a great burden – but you will not carry it for long.'

Chemile released his breath in a snort. 'Is that the best you can do?'

'Behold the omens!' The tip of the knife pointed, moved. 'The liver is diseased, the lungs fretted, the heart covered with fat. The intestines are convoluted and the bowel not as it should be

You have come in haste and fill the shoes of one departed. Of your party you are the head.'

'Repetition,' said Luden softly. 'He has already said that and anyone could arrive at a similar conclusion. You are an obvious stranger and so must have traveled through space. It is easy to tell that you are in command. A pity, I had hoped for something more definite.'

'You face enemies,' droned the augur. 'Beware of birds which walk like men. A smiling face will hide a vengeful heart. Look not too long at beauty. Yet all warnings will be of no avail – in the entrails of this creature lies your fate. Death walks beside you.'

Kennedy said flatly, 'As it does us all.'

'True – but to some it comes before expected. And there will be signs. A room filled with crawling reptiles. Hollows where none should be. A dead voice talking. This I have seen. And more.' Shemarh lifted his head and stared at Kennedy with smoldering eyes. 'I see your body lying on a bier in the palace. Within three days you will be dead.'

CHAPTER FOUR

They entered the palace by a side door, climbing stairs worn hollow with use and time, entering rooms decorated with golden lizards set against a background of scarlet.

'A room filled with crawling reptiles,' Luden mused thoughtfully. 'And no stair should be hollow. Interesting, unless you consider the possibility of the augur having foreknowledge of your destination.'

'Shut up, Jarl.' Saratov was uneasy. 'How could a man like that know the decorations of the palace?'

'Seers and augurs are held in high regard on this world,' said Seward. He had been thoughtful since they had left the square. 'And no one would gain the reputation Shemarh has unless he was good at his craft. It's quite possible that he was summoned by Umed Khan at one time or the other.'

Chemile said, 'Are there lizards in every room?'

'No. It is the totem-beast of the present ruler. These used to be his rooms. Now, of course, he uses the main suite.'

'Which are no doubt being decorated with his symbol.' Luden shrugged. 'A simple matter of the use of common sense. The negotiations cannot have been kept secret and rumor is notorious for its speed of dissemination. An outworld stranger, here for an obvious purpose, would inevitably be given quarters in the palace. Shemarh is a clever man, I agree, but his skills lie elsewhere than in augury.'

'I wish I could be sure of that.' Saratov walked around the apartment, brooding. A wide room led to sleeping chambers, a compartment with a sunken bath. Lizards were everywhere,

32

gold against scarlet; even the handles of the doors were shaped as lizards, tails curved, jaws open as if to snatch at unwary fingers.

Kennedy said firmly, 'I'm sure. Now forget about that nonsense in the square. You too, Veem. That's an order.'

Chemile shrugged in his robe. He walked from one room to the other, returning with a compact case. A recorder. He pressed a control and a dead man spoke.

'. . . addendum to previous report. The Chambodian delegation which recently arrived shows signs of determination in getting Jarhen into their zone of control. Despite the orders of the ruler they have made approaches to Nava Sonega in an effort to gain his support. I have, as a counterbalance, made overtures to Denog Wilde who, I suspect, has far greater influence with Umed Khan than is generally supposed. A complete breakdown on both individuals will be completed and forwarded as soon as possible.'

'Ben Hiton,' said Luden. 'A preliminary report for later action. Who is Nava Sonega?'

'A sort of grand vizier. We suspected him of having engineered the accident which resulted in the late ruler's death. Compared to the general beliefs of this world, he is something of a heretic. Certainly, he is intent on forming an alliance with a protective group.'

Saratov frowned. 'A heretic?'

'Certainly.' Luden was, as always, precise. 'A person who holds other than accepted beliefs. And Denog Wilde?'

'A prognosticator, seer, astrologer, magician.' Seward lifted his shoulders. 'A mystic who reads omens, interprets dreams, studies portents, and reads palms. You name it and he does it. Emissary Hiton wanted to gain his support and use his influence on our behalf. Unfortunately, he didn't have time to complete the arrangements.'

A pity, thought Kennedy, but bribery took time when conducted in an atmosphere of intrigue, mistrust, and opposing offers. Especially when Umed Khan had made it clear that no negotiations were to commence until the auspicious hour. Watchful guards would have reported any violation, and Hiton had been too old a hand at the game to risk all by a careless move.

He said, 'Tell me how he died. Did you find him?'

'No. Armand Blois did that. He went in to wake him with a

33

cup of tisane and found him dead. I sent him with the body to MALACA Eight,' he explained. 'There was to have been three of us – that's another problem.'

'Three.' Luden nodded. 'The Essential Triad. Inevitable when you think about it. The number three has a special esoteric importance,' he explained. 'As does five, seven, eleven, and thirteen. The basic primes. Three delegations consisting each of three members. As you say, young man, that is a problem, but one which can easily be solved. Did you see Hiton before he was moved?'

Seward nodded. 'He looked horrible. He was on his back, mouth open, eyes bulging, throat knotted, and hands tightly clenched. I reached for his shoulder and turned him a little – that's when I saw the water gushing from his mouth. He was full of it. It had killed him.'

'A point,' said Kennedy. 'The bedclothes were perfectly dry? You're sure of it?'

'Positive; his nightwear too. The bed got wet when we moved him, but it was dry at the beginning.'

'Did anyone enter his room?' rumbled Saratov.

'No. The outer door was locked and there was no sign of forced entry.'

'Which means little,' mused Luden. 'This place could be full of secret passages. Was anything unusual found in his chamber? Something you would not have expected to find?'

'Only this.' From a pocket Seward produced a stone. It was the size of a small egg, cut in a number of facets and made of some dull, yellow material. 'This had slipped into the pocket of his pajamas – or he had most probably put it there. I found it when preparing the body for freeze.'

Kennedy reached out and took the stone. It felt cold and slick beneath his fingers. As a gem it was useless, a thing without life or fire despite the facets; no woman would think of wearing it as an adornment. He wondered where Hiton had got it.

'Not from a shop in the city.' Seward was positive as he answered the question. 'Either Armand or myself was in constant attendance and he bought nothing. In fact, he spent all of his time in the palace. Someone could have given it to him, I suppose, but if so he never mentioned it.'

An addition to the mystery of how a man could drown while lying safely in bed. Kennedy tossed the stone, catching it, his eyes thoughtful. Through the thick walls of the palace he could sense rather than hear the pulse of drums, the thudding rhythm of ancient ceremony. At the other side of the chamber, far from where Kennedy stood beside the door, Chemile lifted a warning hand.

'Someone's out there, Cap. Listening, perhaps.'

'Open it, Veem.'

Chemile's ears were sharp. The girl outside had barely time to straighten from where she had crouched with her ear to the opening of the lock. Even so she was quick to regain her composure.

'My lord.' She bowed to Kennedy. 'I come to ask if there is anything you need. Wine, cakes, scents for your bath, attendants to serve you. Your wishes are my command.'

He gestured for her to enter and stand before him.

'My lord?'

She stood, very tall, the long lines of her thighs gleaming through the stranded material of her short skirt. Her feet were bare, the nails painted a burnished gold, more gold on the nails of her fingers, yet more tracing the outline of her lips. Her breasts were bare, tipped with gold, and a thin shining chain bearing the weight of a charm was suspended between them. It was of hammered metal bearing a familiar sign.

'Cap!' Luden's whisper was harsh. 'That's the Zheltyana Seal!'

Kennedy made no effort to touch it. Instead, he stared into the eyes wide spaced beneath arching brows. From the passage outside the golden light from a lantern threw glimmers of gold on the burnished jet of her hair. The eyes were ovoid, the irises flecked with motes of crimson.

Flatly he said, 'The charm, girl. Where did you get it?'

'This?' Slender fingers lifted to the weight around her throat. 'From my mother, my lord, given to me when reaching womanhood. As she received it from her mother, and back from mother to daughter for as long as memory. It gives protection and brings good fortune.'

'Yes,' he said. 'To the extent of a thousand zesh. Yours if you sell it to me.'

'My lord!' She began to tremble, eyes dilating with fear. 'No, my lord! It cannot be!'

'Ten thousand.'

'I – I cannot, my lord. I dare not.'

'Enough for a farm,' urged Kennedy. 'A house in the city,

For a husband and the children you will have. A life of comfort and ease. Twenty thousand zesh if you will sell me your charm.'

He saw the indecision, the conflict which distorted her face, saw too the barely concealed shock and disgust. On Jarhen people did not trade their charms. The disgust was for the temptation she felt, the self-horror at even considering betraying her forebears.

Quickly he said, 'Who ordered you to spy?'

'Rem Naryan. He promised me – ' She broke off, conscious of what she had been saying, and yet she'd had no choice. Kennedy had left her none. Deliberately he had placed her in a dilemma, and equally deliberately had shown her a way out.

Gently he said, 'The Chambodian who leads their delegation?'

'Yes, my lord.'

'On us and others?' There was no need of an answer; he read it in her eyes. He said, 'You will bring us wine. The best in an unopened bottle, and you will say nothing of this to anyone. You understand?'

'My lord!'

She bowed and backed toward the open door. Chemile closed it after her. He said, 'Those damned vultures. Trust them to play dirty.'

'It's a dirty game,' said Kennedy mildly. He wasn't surprised; each delegation would want to learn what it could from the others. If the Chambodians had hired serving girls to spy, it was a fair bet the Inchonians had also. But it had been a clumsy move. Too clumsy. He said, 'Penza. A seal.'

Saratov was already at work. From beneath his loose garment he took a wide belt ringed with pockets. Instruments and components appeared to be rapidly assembled. Within minutes a small device stood on a low table. A touch and it emitted a thin whine which rose above audibility.

'Done, Cap. A sonic barrier for eavesdroppers and an electronic shield against any form of bug and spy-eye. If anyone planted a microphone in here, he's got a bad case of earache by now. If they're watching, they'll see nothing but flashes.'

Seward said, 'I should have taken precautions, but after the Emissary died there seemed little point. I was alone.'

And he was not, thought Kennedy, a man to vocalize his thoughts.

'A pity you could not buy that charm, Cap.' Luden was engrossed by what he had seen. 'The Zheltyana Seal was

36

unmistakable. I would like to give it a radio-active test for age.'

'It would prove nothing.' Kennedy stood, recalling the incident, seeing again in his mental vision the heavy charm against the naked skin of the girl's torso. The convoluted, interwound circles which he knew so well had not been as sharp and regular as they should. The metal would have worn, of course, but that was not the complete answer. 'It was a copy, Jarl. A pattern taken from something else which, in turn, could also have been a copy. And it could have been taken from a device worn by some other race who had found it in turn. It tells us nothing we did not know before.'

'Even so – ' Luden broke off as someone knocked on the door. It was the girl returning with the wine, a tall bottle of cut glass resting on a tray together with three goblets. The bottle was sealed with a blob of wax dry and brittle with age.

'The wine, my lord.'

She had not come alone. Two guards, tall in crested helmets and brazen armor, curved swords naked in their hands, stood to each side of the portal. Between them strode a man, the embroidered brightness of his robe accentuating the aged tautness of his face. He said, without preamble, 'I am Nava Sonega. Welcome to Jarhen.'

Kennedy studied him as Seward made the introductions. The man was old, but there was nothing weak about him. The eyes, slightly upturned, creased with tiny lines, were clear and bright with intelligence. The mouth was thin and bloodless, the jaw a firm line of bone. His forehead was high, the temples hollowed, sweeping back into a peaked skull thinly covered with silver hair.

'Captain Kennedy,' he said thoughtfully. 'The Lord of Sergan. Are you then a noble of that world?'

'No,' said Kennedy flatly. 'The ruler.'

A position won with blood and pain, but useful now in this society which placed high regard on titles. Impressed, Nava Sonega bowed. Terran Control must value Jarhen highly to have sent the ruler of a world to negotiate.

He said, 'We are gratified, my lord, but, with respect, there is a matter of importance. Your delegation should consist of only three members.' His eyes darted to where the other stood. 'Your number is too large – you will correct it?'

Without turning his head Kennedy said, 'Chemile, take Seward and return to the *Mordain*. You understand?'

37

'Yes, Cap.'

For a moment Seward looked as if he would argue, then, shrugging, he followed the cowled figure through the door and into the passage. He would stay in the ship; Chemile would not. Using his special talents, Chemile would return, invisible to searching eyes.

As they left, Kennedy said, 'When shall I have the pleasure of meeting your ruler?'

'Very soon now. Tugool nears the zenith, and when it does, we shall commence. Be at your ease, my lord. You will be summoned.'

Nava Sonega bowed again and, turning, left the room. As the doors closed, Saratov blew out his breath.

'That's the mainspring, Cap. The real power behind the throne. Win him over and the job is done.'

'I doubt it.' Luden was less convinced. 'Even though he may be a heretic as regards the beliefs of this world, he will be held by tradition and the mores of his culture. Umed Khan is, in a sense, a god-king. His word is law. Sonega can only work within a very limited zone of operations.'

'But enough to kill the previous ruler, Jarl.'

'Barely, Penza. We can assume that he managed to cause the cartridge to misfire – tampering with the primer would have done that – but even so he took a chance. Umed Khan could have destroyed both him and the attendants. He could have examined the cartridge. As it was, he believed that fate had given him the rule of this world. A convenient belief, perhaps, but Sonega had to incorporate it into his plan. And so many things could have gone wrong. No, Penza, from our viewpoint the assassination was a clumsy affair.'

'And Nava Sonega didn't strike me as being a clumsy man,' said Kennedy. 'He did the best he could within his limitations. He may be for us, but we still have to convince the ruler.'

Picking up the bottle, Kennedy broke the seal and poured out some of the contents. Cautiously he tasted it. The wine was thick, heavy, cloying to the tongue with a strange aftertaste which could have been the result of herbs. Deliberately he took the bottle into the bathroom and poured the contents down the drain.

Saratov, watching, said, 'Drugged, Cap?'

'I doubt it, but we'll take no chances.' Kennedy tipped what he had poured into the other goblets, swirling them to give the impression they had been used. 'We're going to need clear heads at the conference. If he's like his vizier, Umed Khan is a clever man.'

CHAPTER FIVE

All night the drums had pounded, the heavy rhythm rising from the city to be caught by the wind that always blew at night, to be reflected from towers and turrets and curtain walls of stone, magnified until the very floor on which he stood seemed to vibrate in sympathy, the palace itself, even the world.

There was magic in it, thought Umed Khan. A summons to unknown powers to wake and turn their attention to the destiny of Jarhen. A battering ram of repetitious sound to weaken the veils which hid the future. An instrument of a science as old as time itself used at every spring equinox to ensure good crops, used now to bolster this most auspicious of occasions.

He straightened a little, conscious of his fate, feeling the heady euphoria of a man who has no doubts. He had the tingling, exciting intoxication of one who knows he simply cannot lose, his time has come, luck rides on his shoulder, and nothing can go wrong. And portents were everywhere. In the great square a woman had given birth to a son marked with a lizard, the blotch of the birthmark immediately recognizable. On the shore a leviathan had gasped out its life, easy food for nearby villagers. The trail of the comet had cut through the House of Fire and water had been found at an arid place in the desert.

And even the wind seemed to be more than a natural movement of air. Here, on the platform of the highest tower of the palace, it seemed to hold voices, whispers, subdued murmurs, and now, carrying the throb of the drums, it seemed to shout a paean.

'My lord, it is late.' Nava Sonega moved forward from where he had stood watching beside ancient instruments of wood and brass. 'Your guests should not be kept waiting.'

'There is time.'

'Even so, my lord – '

'There is time,' repeated Umed Khan firmly. He glanced at the sky to reassure himself. Tugool was not yet at zenith, he had a little leeway, and when, really, should the confrontation begin? When he actually met the delegates or when he commenced his journey toward them? A small point, but it could be important. Vaguely he wished that he had consulted Denog Wilde on the matter. He said, 'You are too concerned, Nava. To wait is to our advantage.'

And, waiting, he could receive a sign.

One would come, he was certain of it. The fates which had directed his life would not fail to guide his destiny now. His destiny and that of his world. The path they should take, the choice they would make. A falling star, perhaps? A shift of wind? A vessel of space descending to land? Automatically he divided the sky into three sections, giving each a name. Chambodia, Inchon, Terra, the areas in which their domains lay. A meteor, perhaps, would give the answer.

None came. The sky remained as it was, points of light, curtains of luminescence, the pattern unbroken by any point of falling brilliance.

'My lord.' With an effort Sonega restrained his impatience. 'Already men will be summoning the delegates.'

'A moment.'

Umed Khan looked down at the city. Below, the lanterns of the festival shone with glimmers of red and green, orange and violet, yellow and golden amber. As he stared they seemed to blur, to shift and to form a near-recognizable pattern. A word, perhaps. A sign of mystic significance.

'Nava!'

'My lord?'

'Can you see – ' Umed lifted an arm, pointing. 'The lanterns – '

'Are lanterns, my lord, nothing more.' The dry voice held a note of asperity as Sonega joined the other at the parapet. He added, 'The Lord of Jarhen should not look for symbols in everything he sees.'

A rebuke and one his father would have returned with harshness, his brother too – blinded men begged before mansions they had once owned. But Sonega had earned the right to comment.

He said flatly, 'There is a saying, Nava. There are none so blind as those who will not see.'

'True, my lord.'

'And I have cause to value symbols.'

'Even so, my lord, but with respect, the decision which has to be made is too important to be left to the vagaries of augurs or the influence of omens. As well toss a coin to determine which alliance we shall make – but a world is not a gambler's stake.'

'There are those who would argue that point, Nava.'

'Denog Wilde for one,' agreed Sonega. 'But he and those like him are not the ones who will suffer should the wager be lost.' The dry voice held a note of hard determination. 'Go into the streets, my lord. Look at your people. They are the ones who must pay.'

And who would pay if he misread the portents? For a long moment Umed Khan stood, looking down at the city, remembering the poverty shielded behind walls of moldering stone, the ignorance and disease. As yet fate had not been kind to Jarhen. Lifting his face, Umed stared at the heavens. Tugool was at zenith. It was time.

And still there had been no sign.

Reluctantly he walked toward the stairs, the winding flights which would carry him below to the great audience chamber.

Perhaps he would see something on the journey. A small thing to a casual eye, but which could have great meaning to a man seeking guidance. Not all portents were large; augurs could be read from the body of a mouse as well as the vitals of a drell. He had to remain aware, alert for when it came. At the foot of the stairs a man stood, waiting.

Bowing, he said, 'My lord.'

Sonega was harsh. 'We have no time. Why have you left your cell?'

'News, my lord.' Denog Wilde did not look at the vizier. Instead he raised a hand in a mystic gesture. Like his face it was ghostly pale, the nails bloodless patches of nacre tipping the slender points. His hair, long and fine, was silver, his slanted eyes a disturbing pink. An albino from an island in the Qendle Sea. A mutated sport to whom natural sunlight was an affliction and who spent his days in underground chambers. 'It touches a stranger within the palace.'

42

'A stranger? One of the delegates?'

'It can be no other. A tall man, dressed in black and gold, hard of face, firm of mouth, eyes that see more than is presented. He has a companion wearing a magician's robe, another old, a third grossly fat, a fourth younger, the companion of one now dead.'

'The Lord of Sergan,' said Nava Sonega. It could be none other. 'Captain Kennedy, the head of the delegation from the Terran Sphere. What about him?'

'Shemarh read his fate in the entrails of a beast. Within three days he will be dead.'

An omen? Umed Khan stood, thinking. The workings of fate were mysterious, the portents, at times, hard to read. Should he place the future of his world in the hands of a man doomed to early extinction? Already one member of the Terran delegation had died and now another would follow. Warnings, perhaps?

It was as if Sonega had read his mind. 'My lord, men die and the Lord of Sergan is not yet dead. It could be that the augur was mistaken and that – '

'Shemarh is a master of his craft,' interrupted the albino. 'Never is he wrong.'

' – the omens, if that is what they are, mean other than what they appear.' Sonega ignored the interruption. 'A man has died a sacrifice to destiny. Another is to die and with him will die all the misery and pain of Jarhen. As he will be reborn in some brighter place so this world will be reborn to a new and shining future.'

Denog Wilde said, acidly, 'You speak as though you have already decided the fate of Jarhen.'

'Only one man can do that.' Sonega bowed toward his lord. 'I offer guidance, nothing more.'

'As do I.'

'Perhaps.' It was hard for the vizier to mask his dislike. The albino had a vested interest in maintaining the present status of his world. 'How did you learn of what occurred in the square?'

'Did I mention the square?'

'Shemarh practices there during festival. How did you know?'

A veil seemed to fall over the staring pink eyes. Watching him, Sonega was reminded of something wet and slimy, a creature which lived in the dark places beneath stones.

'I know,' said Denog Wilde after an aching silence. 'Let us say that the stones murmured to me of what had passed. Or

43

perhaps I saw it in my crystal ball. Or read it days ago in the pattern of the stars. Does my lord doubt the truth of what I say?'

He wouldn't have lied, not when the truth could be discovered so easily. Uneasily Umed Khan shook his head. He had yearned for an omen and one had been presented to him – but how should it be read? Both Denog and Nava had given their interpretation and both could be right. To place the fate of Jarhen in hands fated for early death could mean disaster or rebirth. How to decide?

Again Sonega seemed to read his mind.

'My lord, the auguries were made before Tugool reached zenith. In that case they can have little effect on the decision you must make. The auspicious time had not yet arrived. With respect I suggest that only, as from now, should portents be considered of immediate value.'

A good point, immediately counterbalanced by the albino.

'You have only just received the news, my lord. It is past the zenith of Tugool.'

'The event is old,' snapped Sonega. 'The Lord of Jarhen cannot be influenced by stale news.'

'Fate has delayed it,' murmured the albino. 'And who can guess for what purpose?'

'Enough!' Umed Khan was tired of the bickering. Balance and counterbalance had destroyed the value of the portent; once more he was without guidance.

Smoothly Sonega said, 'The Triad should not be broken. Auguries should be read for all, not one. Alone they are value-less.'

A hint which the ruler was quick to grasp. To the albino he said, 'They are strangers from other worlds. Born under different suns. Is your skill great enough to read their fates and align them to mine?'

For a moment Denog Wilde hesitated, then admitted a partial defeat. 'No, my lord, but we can work on other things than planets of birth and stars of determination. There are tests and devices, hard but not impossible. Is it your wish – '

'No,' snapped Sonega. Events were taking a turn which he did not like. 'We deal with high-placed lords of powerful combines. They will not be willing to play foolish games.'

He had gone too far and immediately he knew it; trapped by his heresy he had denigrated the very basis of Jarhenian

44

life. There was nothing foolish about spells, amulets, and a
belief in fate. A lucky charm worked – the continued existence
of the wearer proved it. Fate was real and could be seen working
all the time – how else to account for coincidences, accidents,
strokes of unexpected good fortune? Portents had meaning,
omens were expressive, augurs were significant: all were sign-
posts no sensible person would ignore.

Quickly he said, 'Foolish to them, of course. Their ways are
not ours. And, my lord, they are waiting.'

Denog Wilde said quietly, 'My lord, the Jewel?'

Umed Khan squared his shoulders. Sonega could be forgiven;
old and worried, he had momentarily lost control, a lapse he
could forget now that the albino had shown him a possible
answer.

The Jewel of Jarhen, the mystic gem that now reposed in the
vaults, the stone that, so legend had it, had been handed down
to the first ruler by visitors from the stars. The legend probably
lied, but the jewel held power. Power enough, perhaps, to provide a solution to the problem still to be faced.

He would not use it, he promised himself. Sacred treasure
should not be displayed to unappreciative eyes. It would be a
last resort and he would try all else first.

'Return to your cell,' he told the albino. 'Cast the pattern of
my stars. Tugool has just passed zenith, Argoon is in aspect and
Sponel is in trine. The comet now in the House of Fire may
have created a complication in the eighth cusp. And the augur
' approaching death to one of the delegates may have
influenced what-is-to-be. If so, I must know it. Go.'

Sonega said as the man hurried away, 'We shall have no
need of the Jewel, my lord. It will be a matter of listening,
questioning, balancing one advantage against another. The
delegates are representative of their races; from them we can
learn all we need to know.'

'Men can lie, Nava.'

'And pacts be signed, my lord.'

'And later broken.' Umed Khan shrugged. 'And what then?
Can Jarhen resist the pressure of aggression should it come?
Have we ships and men skilled in the art of spacial war? No,
Nava, we must be certain of what we do. The destiny of a
world is not to be risked on a smile that hides falsehood.'

He led the way down the passage to where a door opened on
a wide corridor, guards snapping to attention as he approached,

45

the ruddy glow of flambeaux glinting on brazen armor, crested helmets, the writhing gold of lizards on scarlet backgrounds, the tips of pikes and the shimmering edges of naked swords. Ornamented panels swung open as they advanced, tall leaves carved with mystic symbols, patterns designed to ensure truth and good fortune, parting to show the chamber beyond, the men standing at the far edge of the curved table before which stood the chair of state. The sound of a gong thundered as Umed Khan stepped toward it, echoing from the groined roof to fade in whispering murmurs as he sat.

Barbaric splendor to herald the birth of a new age. The conference had begun.

CHAPTER SIX

Kennedy had expected to be bored. He had no love for the tedium of diplomatic maneuvering, the endless talk, the half-truths, the searching for hidden meanings in apparently innocuous statements, the striving for personal advantage in ceaseless verbal manipulations. It was a game he could play if he had to, and play it well, but he preferred the more familiar route of direct action. Now he was pleasantly surprised.

Umed Khan was responsible for that. Sitting at the right of the table, flanked by Luden and Saratov, Kennedy studied the ruler of Jarhen. A big man, rotund beneath his robe of state, his face heavy, the jowls prominent, the eyes hooded beneath jutting brows. A strong face which had early learned how to mask inward emotion. A clever man also to have survived in a culture which did not tolerate younger sons and the threat they represented to the one in power.

A little to Umed's rear, seated at his left in a position where he could talk without being overheard, Nava Sonega was an attendant shadow. A strong combination, shrewd and fighting for their world. Kennedy never made the mistake of underestimating his opponents, and these men, barbaric though they might appear, were far from stupid.

And neither were the others.

Kennedy turned his attention to Thom Ochran. The Inchonian was on his feet, a squat man, his face flattened, his nostrils flared beneath prominent eyes. His ears were pointed, tufted with a fine down, more down on face and hands. His hair was long, lifting to a high ridge so that he resembled, at a quick glance, a Pekingese. His attendants were younger, their fur darker, glowing in the light of the lanterns which threw a golden circle over the table. He had spoken before, Umed Khan cutting short his lengthy exposition; now he was elaborating in the light of what the others had said.

Luden whispered, 'He's making a mistake, Cap. He's gilding the lily.'

Kennedy nodded, listening. Jarhen would become a member of the Inchonian Enclave. Full protection would be offered against outside aggression. Traders would be sent to offer manufactured goods for sale. Industries would be established, schools opened, work provided. All this he had said before, but now there was more. Full citizen status would be granted to those able to prove their worth. An involved system of credit would be established, local authority respected, reciprocal trade agreements formulated.

Leaning forward, Nava Sonega whispered to the ruler. Umed Khan held up a hand.

'Enough. Why did you not say this before?'

'My lord?'

'You mention full citizen status. How will my people be able to prove their worth?'

'A simple examination, my lord, based on knowledge and intelligence.'

'Who will decide the standards?'

Thom Ochran was an honest man. 'We will, my lord. But the advantages to you will be immense. Once the pact is signed we will send an argosy of vessels to offer you the products of our industry. Openings will be made for selected persons to work in our factories. Within a generation Jarhen will be equal to any other world in the Inchonian Enclave. And, as proof of our good intent, a balance of five million zesh will be placed at your disposal for the purchase of any goods you may deem necessary.'

'Credit, not cash?'

'Credit, my lord.'

Saratov rumbled deep in his chest. 'As Weyburn said, Cap. They're after a new market and cheap labor, but he's honest about it, or as honest as a diplomat can be. We can top him.'

'It isn't as easy as that, Penza,' whispered Luden sharply. 'We're up against superstition. Something, I think, the Chambodian hasn't taken into account.'

48

Rem Naryan rose, tall, proud, arrogant in a manner he made no attempt to disguise. His face was wedge-shaped, the nose beaked, the mouth a slit above a sloping jaw. His eyes, deep-set, were slanted, the irises horizontal slots. The product of a race which had evolved from avian stock. His hands were like claws, the nails sharp, inwardly curved, the scaled knuckles prominent.

Acidly he said, 'The Chambodian Complex offers to lead this world into the future. We shall protect you and teach you to exploit your wealth. Under our guidance you will become rich and powerful – but these things you know. Consider the alternative. The helpless slaves of an industrial organization that is interested only in selling you cheap and unwanted goods and obtaining a supply of inexpensive labor with the vague promise that, one day, you may be admitted to equal status. Or – ' he turned to glance at Kennedy – 'to belong to a decadent assembly of worlds which constitutes the Terran Sphere. An assembly which promises little aside from a dubious protection and aid should you need it. Chambodia does not come as a beggar after favors – instead we come as a strong power willing to accept Jarhen into our Complex. We offer no bribe, instead we give you the chance to share in our great destiny.'

A good touch, thought Kennedy, an appeal to the very fabric on which Jarhenian life was based. And barbarians could appreciate the arrogance and conviction of superiority that the Chambodian radiated, the superiority of a race that hated and despised the monkey-men of other worlds.

Rising, Kennedy said, 'Vague words, my lord, and without meaning. I deal in facts. Join the Terran Sphere and no demands of any kind will be made. There will be free intercourse between our peoples. Trade and industry will follow. Aid given, at your request only, if you decide you need it. Your customs respected and your authority maintained. And,' he added meaningfully, 'should other powers encroach on your domain they will be utterly destroyed.'

Umed Khan sighed; he had learned nothing new. As Kennedy sat down he turned to Sonega. The vizier leaned close.

'A time for refreshment, my lord,' he whispered. 'And a time for thought. The discussion could be endless. We have heard all there is to hear – now you must ponder your decision.'

It was a decision Umed Khan found impossible to make. He leaned back as serving girls came forward with trays bearing

49

wine and cakes, summoned by the sonorous beat of a gong. The Chambodian radiated power, the Inchonian honesty, the Terran both. He sat, brooding, watching Kennedy, wondering how it must feel to know the approach of death. Three days the augur had said, but always there was a margin of doubt. Three days was the maximum, the man could die now, before his very eyes. Would his decision bring about that end? Would he live only until the pact had been signed?

Looking up, Kennedy met his eyes. Flatly he said, 'My lord, if you are in doubt, there is a way to settle the question. Jarhen will not wish to be aligned with the weak. If the others are willing, let personal combat decide.'

Sonega frowned. 'A custom of your world?'

'At one time, yes. Fate will dictate who is in the right.'

A tempting proposition, and Umed Khan considered it, then reluctantly shook his head. Kennedy was young, the others old; in battle he would hold the advantage. And if the attendants should fight, the bulk of one would more than compensate for the fragility of the other.

Luden said quietly, 'A good try, Cap.'

'Not good enough.'

'But you appealed to their barbaric instincts as well as their superstitions. For a moment the Chambodian was worried.' Luden glanced at the Chambodian, who was toying with a goblet of wine. 'What puzzles me is why they should want this world at all. It's far from the edge of their Complex and doesn't seem to be worth the bother. They want to get back at us, of course, but they aren't stupid. To create a node of discord wouldn't be worth the disadvantage of having to maintain lines of communication and the inevitable trouble once they install a governor and the usual military establishment.' Luden nibbled delicately at a cake. 'There must be another reason, and I'm inclined to think it may have something to do with Hiton's death.'

'Maybe Rem Naryan wanted to knock out the competition,' Kennedy suggested.

'Then why isn't the Inchonian dead?' Luden frowned, thinking. 'Maybe he was due and our arrival spoiled the plan. Or perhaps they have arrived at some arrangement. He didn't appear to put his case in the best light. And yet, in these circumstances, how is it possible to tell?' He bit again at the cake, a little annoyed with himself for his own lack of precision. A man of science, he would rather not deal with those who were more concerned with lucky charms and portents than in-controvertible fact. There were too many intangibles; the path of an insect could determine the fate of a world, it was impossible to be sure.

Kennedy said, 'We're heading toward an impasse. I'm going to try something.' Rising, he looked at the ruler. 'My lord, you have heard all of us and what we propose. A trial of strength would determine the instrument of fate, but that you disallow. There is another way. The Chambodian lies. The Inchonian does not lie, but has not stated the whole truth. This I can prove.'

Intrigued, Umed Khan said, 'How?'

'Hot metal placed on the tongue will burn a liar, but not injure an honest man. I am willing to take the test. Let a brazier be brought and a knife placed in the coals. When it is red-hot we shall begin.'

'A trick,' snapped Rem Naryan quickly. 'No Terran can be trusted.'

Kennedy said, dangerously, 'Are you calling me a liar?'

'And if I am?'

'There are three of you. I will fight alone.'

'Please, gentlemen.' Thom Ochran was disturbed. This was not the way diplomatic negotiations should be conducted. 'You forget who you are and why you are here.'

Kennedy ignored him. 'My lord?'

Again Umed Khan reluctantly shook his head. His barbaric nature could appreciate the proposal, but what did a man fated to die have to lose? And there was a better way.

To Nava Sonega he said, 'Go and bring the Jewel.'

'But – '

'At once! How else can we decide?'

It came in a box thick with gold, studded with gems sparkling with a myriad hues. The light from the lanterns caught it and covered it with rainbow shimmers, spectrums of brilliance turning the wood into a living thing. Resting his hand on the lid, Umed Khan faced the delegates.

'You are from other worlds and have other ways, but now you are on Jarhen and the customs we follow are the ones you must obey. Long, long ago this Jewel was given to one who ruled. It contains a great magic, and in it are held the threads of destiny. Look into it. Repeat your proposals. If you mean what

51

you say, there will be nothing to fear. If you have lied, I shall know it.'

Luden said softly, 'I don't like this, Cap. If he has a lie detector, why hasn't he used it before? It can't be anything as simple as that.'

Thom Ochran cleared his throat. 'How will you know it, my lord?'

The Chambodian was more direct. 'Am I a slave to be put to the question? To doubt my word is to throw doubt on the race to which I belong. Such an insult cannot be borne.' He turned, his elbow catching his goblet, spilling it so that wine gushed in a puddle on the table. It formed the amorphous shape of a man.

Umed Khan stared at it as a serving girl hurried to clear up the mess. An omen? The shape of a man could mean that he should turn to the Terran or, again, it could mean that the Chambodian was dominant. How to be sure? The box beneath his hand gave the answer. Denog Wilde had mentioned it, and who could tell what had prompted his words?

He said harshly, 'I am the Lord of Jarhen. I will be obeyed. Go if you wish – but if you do, this world will never follow your star.'

Rem Naryan hesitated. The thin, hawk-face was a mask, but Kennedy could sense the turmoil within. Should he fail without just cause his superiors would not be gentle. He would lose rank, privilege, his birth-egg ceremoniously destroyed, his family dishonored. Misplaced pride, now, would cost him dear.

Umed Khan opened the box.

Inside rested the living heart of a star.

Immediately Kennedy corrected the impression, one born of the tide of living effulgence that had poured from the open container, dimming the golden light of the lanterns. Not the heart of a star but a jewel, as large as his clenched fist, cut with a multitude of facets and resting on a bed of ebon substance like jet. It shone with a lambent yellow, almost hurtful to the eyes so that he squinted, seeing from beneath lowered lids the shape of the thing the box contained.

Not a jewel as implied by the usual meaning. It had never been made to wear. There was a peculiar asymmetry about it, oddly mechanical, a mathematical combination of lines and planes following the dictates of an involved equation. Even the facets were irregular, as if cut to a complex pattern.

Luden whispered, 'Cap! That's an artifact of some kind.'

It was a machine or a part of a machine the original purpose of which had long been forgotten. Looking at it, Saratov felt a sudden dread. Ever since the prediction in the square that dread had been growing. The warnings had been followed too close, the hollows where none should have been, the room filled with reptiles, the voice of a man now dead. Almost he could hear the thin voice of the augur.

Beware of birds which walk like men. A smiling face will hold a vengeful heart. Look not too long at beauty.

Chambodians were birds that walked like men. And Rem Naryan's thin smile held nothing gracious as he turned from the table to whisper to one of his aides. And Kennedy was staring too hard and too long at the beauty of the Jewel.

There had been other things of beauty. The serving girls who had lingered before the tall Terran, boldly trying to catch his attention, their eyes wide with admiration. Their skin had been like velvet beneath the glow of the lanterns, lithe with animal grace, and Kennedy had stared back, human enough to appreciate what he saw. But Saratov had known Kennedy would never forget the importance of the task in hand, and if one of them was an assassin, he would not allow her to get close enough to strike.

The warning, then, must apply to the Jewel.

Saratov edged closer, one hand thrust into his pocket, feeling the ornament he had bought in the square beneath his fingers. Idly he fumbled with the wires, the inset stones, barely conscious of what he was doing.

'Cap!' he said. 'Cap, be careful!'

Kennedy barely heard him as he concentrated on the Jewel. Jarl was right, he thought, the thing was a mechanical construct and, intrigued, he leaned closer, wishing he had a filter, something to cut the glare. It came from a power-source of some kind, he guessed, and wondered how the thing would operate. Turn red at a lie, perhaps? Delicate sensors could pick up mental emissions and correlate conscious statements with subconscious intentions. Language would be no barrier, the microelectric disturbance would be enough if the device was sensitive. Would bodily contact have to be made?

'Look into the Jewel,' intoned Umed Khan. 'Stare into its heart. Answer when I speak.'

Bodily contact was unnecessary then. Kennedy fought the urge to pick up the box and examine what it contained more

53

closely. Later, perhaps, after the job was done, there might be a chance. In the meantime he hoped Luden was making the most of the opportunity.

Saratov gave him little chance. His big hand gripped the thin arm and, as Luden turned, frowning, he whispered, 'I don't like this, Jarl. Remember that augur? Cap's taking a risk.'

'Nonsense, Penza!'

'Everything else came as he predicted. The lizards, the dead voice, the birds like men.' He glared at the Chambodian delegation. Rem Naryan, he noted, was not staring at the Jewel. 'I don't trust that character.'

'What can he do? Umed Khan said that if the truth were spoken, no harm would come to the one speaking it. Cap isn't going to lie.'

Saratov glanced at Kennedy. 'I just don't like it,' he insisted. 'I keep thinking of Hiton and the way he died. If it happened once, it could happen again.'

'I doubt it, Penza.' Luden was impatient. 'As we don't know what happened to Ben Hiton, it is impossible to make such a statement. Cap is perfectly safe here. We are with him and, in any case, he can look after himself. Now I really must return to my examination of the Jewel.'

Saratov let him go, admitting defeat, trying to ignore the prickling of his skin, the old, familiar warning of impending danger. Bleakly he looked around. The serving girls had gone, the guards also, unfit to look at the sacred stone. Rem Naryan had joined the other two delegates, shouldering aside Luden and taking his place to one side of the Inchonian. He was not, Saratov noted, looking into the box and neither were his two aides. The Inchonians, too, seemed preoccupied.

Nervously Saratov dug his hand into his pocket and found the ornament, strong fingers squeezing.

The Jewel pulsed.

A flood of radiance lifted from the box like a cloud, a glare of eye-bright brilliance which painted every detail in golden splendor. It washed over Umed Khan, his vizier, the three figures leaning close. One turned and stepped quickly away. One slumped to lie on the polished wood. The third jerked upright, spun, and toppled to the floor.

'Cap!'

The sound burst from Saratov's chest, a deep bull-roar that rose to the groined roof to be reflected in a thunder of rolling echoes. Before they had died he was on his knees, rising with the limp figure cradled in his massive arms.

'Penza!' Luden turned toward him, face anxious. 'What – '

'Jarl!' His voice broke as Luden hurried to his side. 'It's Cap, Jarl, He's dead!'

CHAPTER SEVEN

The couch was a bier needing only candles at head and foot
to make it an object of tradition. And there should have been
flowers, thought Saratov bitterly. Lilies and waxen blossoms to
fill the air with a sickly stench, incense too, perhaps, and
mourners to wail their grief. The prophecy fulfilled, the auguries
confirmed, everything had come to pass as the old man had
predicted.

Almost.

'Physically he is alive,' said Luden tiredly. 'Heartbeat and
respiration as to be expected of a man in deep coma. But I can
gain no trace of mental awareness.'

Saratov said, 'His eyes?'

'Apparently undamaged. I would have expected to find some
burning of the cornea, if not retinal searing, but none is
apparent. Which is odd when you consider how close he was to
the Jewel. The glare, therefore, could not have been purely
physical. I am inclined to believe that it must have been partly
psychic, if not totally. An inward stimulation of the mental
process rather than a purely extraneous manifestation. It could
give us a clue.'

'To get Cap back?'

'Of course.' Luden glanced toward the couch, at the still
figure lying supine. 'That must be our prime objective.'

Chemile said, 'It wouldn't have happened had I been here.'

He had been waiting for them when they had carried Kennedy back to their rooms, slipping from the palace to return to
the *Mordain* for medical supplies, returning to wait as they

worked, Luden deft with his ministrations, Saratov using his great strength to keep the heart beating, the lungs working, restoring a semblance of life to the still body, not stopping until he was sure that, physically at least, Kennedy was alive.

A strange, horrible life, he thought. The body working but without a brain. A human, living vegetable unable to eat or move, unable to do anything but breathe. How long, he wondered, could a man live in such a condition? But he knew the answer. With the correct life-support apparatus such a man could last indefinitely. He looked down at his hands, knotted as they rested on his knees. They were instruments of destruction and revenge, if he could only find a target. But who was to blame?

'I should have been here,' said Chemile again. 'I could have learned something. I could still learn it. Whoever did this to Cap must pay.'

'A stone,' said Luden bleakly. 'An ancient artifact. How can you make it pay, Veem?'

'Someone must have used it. A stone wouldn't just act like that on its own. It would need a trigger of some kind.' Chemile paced the floor, colors writhing over his scaled body, a sure sign that he was mentally disturbed. And yet, like Saratov, he felt helpless. 'Perhaps if we took him back to Earth,' he suggested. 'They might be able to do something.'

'There is nothing they can do that we haven't already done, Veem,' said Luden. 'Physically Cap is in good condition. There are no external or internal injuries. Only his mind has been affected, and I believe that we can do more for him here than we can anywhere else. Somehow he must have received a tremendous psychic shock. I would have said that for a normal man it was one great enough to have forced his mind to attempt to escape. To withdraw into a catatonic condition in which a refuge would be found in a prenatal state. However, in such a case the body would have adopted a fetal position. Cap's body responds to applied stimuli in a normal manner. It is as if his mind had somehow become detached. There are symptoms of a dream-state, as if he were sleeping rather than unconscious. However, it is impossible to waken him by any method I know.'

Saratov said, 'What about the other one?'

'Thom Ochran?'

'He fell the same time as Cap. I remember seeing his men carry him away. If he's alive, maybe they could help us.'

'And what about Nava Sonega?' Saratov rose, eager for action of any kind, for his metabolism made it impossible for him to remain quiescent for long. 'Maybe he'd be willing to answer a few questions. If he isn't – ' He broke off, looking at his hands.

'There are guards,' Luden quietly reminded him. 'And he will be close to the ruler. I think it best that I ask the questions. You discover what you can, Veem. I would suggest you visit the Chambodian quarters.'

'You suspect them, Jarl?'

'Cap was warned to beware of birds who walked like men,' rumbled Saratov. 'And we know they have no love for Terra. If I thought those damned vultures had done this to Cap, I'd tear them apart – slowly.'

'If we had proof of that, Penza, I'd help you to do it,' said Luden grimly. 'You had better remain on guard. If you are ready, Veem?'

They parted outside the chamber, Chemile merging into the walls as a guard passed, the man's eyes passing over him, unsuspecting that a stranger was within the palace. Another guided Luden to where Nava Sonega was to be found.

It was a low-roofed chamber lined with volumes, maps on the walls, a globe resting on a stand of polished wood beside a wide desk littered with reports, fragments of carving, a clutter of various charms, knives, mummified remains, the cruel horn of a drell.

'I share your misfortune,' said the vizier as he gestured his visitor to a chair. 'Fate has seemingly decreed that we shall not form an alliance with those who sent you.'

'Seemingly?'

'We are both men of maturity,' said Sonega obliquely. 'Let us say that the death of another of your delegates presented a bad omen.'

'The Lord of Sergan is not dead. His mind sleeps, that is all.'

'I am gratified to hear it. However, the fact remains, Umed Khan believes the Jewel spoke and guided his hand. Within three days we shall join the Chambodian Complex.'

'It will be a mistake.'

'Naturally, from your point of view,' agreed Nava Sonega. 'From ours? Well, that has yet to be determined. In any case, it is decided. The portents left little choice.' He added, after a pause, 'A pity that fate did not stay its hand. An hour, less, and

58

things could have been otherwise. My master was impressed with your lord.'

'And he will have cause to regret his decision,' said Luden. 'I know the Chambodians, you don't. By the time you have learned it will be too late. However, I didn't come here to discuss that. I came for your help.'

'Ask. What can be given will be supplied.'

'The Jewel. I want to examine it.'

'That cannot be.'

Luden didn't press the point, recognizing the flat determination of the answer. Instead he said, 'Your skill, then. Have you spells or charms to recall a wandering mind?'

For a moment the vizier met his eyes and then, slowly, he smiled. 'Magic is for those who believe,' he said. 'I feel that you do not. Charms?' He gestured toward his cluttered desk. 'Here is more than enough, charms for good luck, for easy childbirth, for protection against disease, for defense against false accusations. Spells? I can give you a hundred incantations. Mystic symbols? Powerful runes? Help yourself.'

'I am serious, Nava Sonega.'

'Your lord means much to you?' Sonega lost his smile. 'I see that he does. Your fate and his are inter-wound. Will you believe me when I tell you there is nothing I can do?'

'Aid can take many forms. The Jewel, for example. Has it acted in this way before?'

'No. If one looks into it and lies the hue changes to red and the liar goes mad. This I have seen. Also, I have seen rulers stare into it for hours as if entranced. They are never the same afterward. They walk as if in a dream and do things which should not be done.'

'Such as having men impaled in the great square. Women, too.' Luden understood. 'Who suggested using the Jewel?'

'Denog Wilde.' A veil dropped over the vizier's eyes. 'A man who claims much skill,' he murmured. 'If any can help you, it would be he.' Reaching out, he touched a gong. 'A guard will take you to his chambers.'

They were low beneath the palace, the walls damp and blotched with lichen, the haunt of things which watched from cracks with beady eyes. Luden found what he expected, pentacles drawn on the flagged stones of the floor, braziers giving heat and light and a scented smoke, mummified creatures resting in shadows, all the appurtenances of mysticism. And yet there was more: objects of crystal and metal finely calibrated, charts drawn with painstaking care, modern star maps, a stellar almanac, spectroscope, Kells which glowed with a steady blue luminescence; the transparent bulbs fluorescing to the action of a pinch of radioactive isotopes.

Strange items to be found on a barbaric world, in a palace lit by flambeaux. Payment for services rendered, perhaps? Gifts from grateful clients? Bribes?

Luden examined a star map and noted the Chambodian symbol. Casually he said, 'I could give you better. Good predictions need accurate information.'

Denog Wilde made no comment. He stood behind a table starkly bare aside from a skull. A vial of amber liquid rested to one side of a dish from which rose a thread of smoke.

'Am I disturbing your labors?'

'The thing is done. What do you want?' He blinked as Luden stated his errand. 'To break the veil needs great preparation and costly items. The danger is not small. To wrest a soul from a body and send it into another place is to challenge the very workings of fate itself. I do not think it possible to aid your lord.'

'I have a magic as great as your own,' said Luden softly. 'With it you can travel the stars and determine the obedience of men. We call it money. And I have another. One which will plunge you into eternal darkness. We call it death. The choice is yours.'

'You threaten me?'

Luden stood, saying nothing, eyes direct as he studied the albino. The man, he guessed, possessed a wild talent, rudimentary telepathy, perhaps, coupled with a degree of predetermination or clairvoyance, something of which he was unconsciously aware and which had set him apart from his fellows as had his lack of pigmentation. In this culture such a man could only become a seer.

Denog Wilde said again, 'You threaten me. I read it in your heart and it shows in your eyes. How could you, an old man hope to defeat one favored of the beings who determine the destiny of worlds?'

Luden raised his right hand. The tiny laser strapped to his wrist made no sound and the weapon did not incorporate the usual red guiding beam. As he flexed his muscles a hole appeared in the skull.

'That could have been your head,' he said mildly. 'Why did you suggest using the Jewel?'

'When all else fails it provides the answer.'

'Did anyone tell you to mention it to Umed Khan?' Luden saw the man's eyes shift to glance at the star map. 'A Chambodian?'

'I thought you came to ask for aid.'

'And you will give it.' Another hole appeared in the skull and Luden's voice became as hard and as brittle as the bone. Frail though his body might appear, there was nothing weak about his mind or courage. 'Talk, damn you! Talk before I burn out your eyes!'

'There was a meeting,' admitted the albino. 'Rem Naryan visited me and gave me certain items.' Again he looked at the map, the calibrated instrument of crystal and metal. 'He professed an interest in my art and sought charms to ensure the success of his mission. He had heard of the Jewel – I told him nothing. He hinted that it might be as well to ensure its use. That is all. I swear it!'

All, but the things unsaid completed the story. The Chambodian was shrewd and had determined the influence the albino had with Umed Khan. They would have talked and the master of diplomacy would have skillfully weaved his web. Flattered by gifts and attentions, Denog Wilde would have been a little careless, a thing now he would never admit.

'I would have urged the use of the Jewel in any case,' he added. 'The lines of fate as determined by the Lord of Jarhen's pattern in the stars made it essential. To have remained silent would have been to fail in my duty.'

Luden said, 'Did you show Rem Naryan the Jewel?'

'No. That was not possible. It is held under strong guard.'

'But he asked?'

'Yes.'

'And you described it, perhaps? Spoke of its use?' The albino's silence was answer enough. And there had been no real need for him to remain reticent. The Jewel would be used, the Chambodian would see it; what harm in anticipating the event? Luden filed away the scant information; now there were matters of greater urgency. He said, 'You know why I came. Can you help me?'

'To restore the mind of your lord to its body?' Denog Wilde shrugged. 'I do not know. You see, I am honest with you. In order to negate a spell the details must be known. A strong charm needs a stronger countercharm. Incantations must not only be nullified but replaced. And the Jewel of Jarhen is the very heart of destiny itself. But I shall do what can be done.'

Picking up the skull, he scowled at the twin holes and threw it petulantly into a corner. From a cabinet he took another and set it with the gaping eye-sockets facing the dish from which rose the thread of smoke. A scatter of dust caused fumes to rise from a brazier, thick coils of pungent smoke which roiled beneath the low roof. With chalk he drew an elaborate sign on the table ringing both dish and skull.

Watching him, Luden thought of the ancient alchemists of Earth with their incantations and mystic symbols. Early chemists who felt their way cautiously through unknown perils, blaming demons when poisonous vapors robbed them of life and strength. And there were parallels, he thought. Call an incantation an equation, a charm, a formula, the coils of smoke an antiseptic, the sign a depiction of an electronic circuit, and perhaps the ways of this world could be made to form a logical pattern. Early photographers had followed a rigid pattern, knowing that only by the use of red light could latent images be developed. Red light, carefully mixed compounds, their formulas muttered perhaps as an essential reminder.

Irritably he shook his head, conscious of his fatigue. Science had no place for superstition, yet here, in this underground chamber, surrounded by mystic appliances, it was tempting to think that perhaps there could be another way than the one he knew to the solution of the problems of the universe.

Carefully Denog Wilde poured the contents of the vial into the dish. The thread of smoke thickened, wreathing his face as he stooped over the container, a veil through which his pink eyes stared like those of a man entranced.

'Think of your lord,' he intoned. 'Call him with your mind.'

On the lambent surface of the liquid within the dish a face appeared.

'Cap!' Luden leaned forward as the image vanished. 'What – ?'

'There are barriers,' murmured Denog Wilde. 'Doubts. My art must not be constrained.'

Again the image appeared, the eyes closed, the muscles slack. A picture taken from his mind by the albino's talent and projected so as to appear on the liquid? Luden had no way of telling. And then, as he watched, the face changed, the flesh vanishing to reveal the skull beneath, that in turn seeming to become transparent to show a tiny glow, a minute spark hovering in a well of darkness.

And, from it, as thin and ghostly as a spider's thread, ran a silver line.

Denog Wilde sobbed deep in his throat, the sound of a man straining, almost at the limits of his strength.

'Hard,' he whispered. 'To follow – so hard. I doubt if it is possible.'

'Try.'

'There is a barrier. I cannot – '

'Try,' snapped Luden again, his eyes on the image in the dish. *Cap*, he thought. *Come back to us, Cap. Come back!*

The image vanished. Rising, Luden saw the albino leaning on the edge of the table. Sweat dewed the pale skin and he breathed with a harsh rasping as if his lungs had been seared with noxious vapors. His eyes were sore, matted with swollen capillaries.

'I can do no more,' he gasped. 'Your lord lives, but in another place. One I cannot discern.'

Shaken, Luden said, 'Can you bring him back?'

'No. The Jewel – ' The albino gulped and walked unsteadily to a cabinet from which he took a vial of ruby liquid. Swallowing it, he leaned against the wall. 'No man can break the power of the Jewel,' he said after a few moments. 'I tried and almost lost my spirit in the attempt. You saw – '

A picture in a dish. An hallucination, perhaps, induced by drugged vapors, Luden couldn't be sure. But Denog Wilde was obviously exhausted and afraid.

'You tried,' said Luden. 'But there are no rewards for failure.'

'You destroyed my skull. It was old and contained great power. The other had not learned to see as far.' The albino pulled himself from the wall and looked at the dish. It was empty. 'And the Fluid of Kaarn is gone. A hundred zesh would not replace it.'

He was recovering, thought Luden, and, charlatan or not, he could still be of use. Dryly he said, 'Call it an investment. When you have succeeded, gifts will be yours.'

'You will teach me the secret of destruction?' The albino glanced at the ruined skull.

'Perhaps.' A laser would make this man supreme among his kind. Invisible death dealt by a pointing finger. 'Money, certainly – and money buys many things. When the Lord of Sergan is himself again he will be generous.

Back in the chamber Luden looked at the still figure. It was as he had left it, heartbeat slow, respiration barely noticeable. The skin was cool beneath his touch. To Saratov he said, 'Has there been any change?'

'No. I thought I saw him twitch, once. A jerk of his cheek, but it could have been the light.'

Luden stooped, examining the eyes, lifting the lids as he used the opthalmoscope Chemile had brought back from the *Mordain.*

Looming anxiously at his side, Saratov said, 'Did you learn anything, Jarl?'

'No, Penza; at least nothing of immediate value. Has anyone tried to get in here?'

'No.' The giant looked at his hands. 'I was hoping one of those vultures would try something. If they had – '

'There'll be time for that later,' interrupted Luden. 'When we are certain. All we can do for now is to wait and learn what we can.'

Wait and stand guard – Saratov would do that – until nature repaired the damage or some other way was found. Looking at Kennedy's lax features, Luden remembered the dish and what he had seen, or thought he had seen. The tiny mote of light and the ghostly thread. If that thread should break, would Kennedy die? Did it lead to the place where his mind had gone?

Saratov rumbled, 'I feel so helpless standing here. If there was only something I could do.'

'There is.' An outlet had to be found for the giant's energy. 'You can give him massage, Penza. Keep his muscles in condition. When Cap wakes he won't thank us if he's weak.'

'I'll do that, Jarl. When he comes back Cap will be as strong as he ever was.'

Comes back? A verbal trick? Luden remembered he had used the same words when seeing the image. Was it that neither of them could bear the thought of final extinction or had they, somehow, instinctively guessed the truth? He turned, baffled, for one of the few times in his life unsure of himself. If only he knew exactly what had happened!

CHAPTER EIGHT

The universe had exploded.

One second Kennedy had been leaning toward the Jewel, eyes narrowed against the light, his agile mind busy extrapolating presented detail: the shape of the stone, the pattern of the facets, a half familiar association nagging at the edge of his consciousness. The next everything was lost in a sudden gush of stunning brilliance, a blaze of effulgence that penetrated into the innermost corners of his brain.

And then he was in water.

It was all around, a tight envelope of constricting liquid, numbing pressure forcing it into his ears, against his eyes, filling his nostrils, and pressing hard against the lips he had instinctively closed. He was deep, only a dim light illuminated the scene, the spined and questing snout of a creature which darted away with a flurry of fins as, automatically, Kennedy struck out for the surface.

He was a good swimmer, in aquatic sports he could hold his own against men trained to water from birth, and the Divers of Oldemah accepted him as their equal, but now he needed all his skill, the massive air-retention capacity of his lungs. The pressure was immense, the shock of transition too great. Another man would have been lost, slow to respond to the new environment. He would have parted his lips, gulped, filled stomach and lungs with water, rising to float, a corpse if he rose at all. Only the hard training over difficult years gave Kennedy the ability to survive.

The light grew brighter, sunlight blazing as he broke the surface to turn, lying on his back as he sucked in great drafts of salt-scented air. He was, he realized, completely naked; another mystery to add to the other. How he had come here, thrown instantly from the audience chamber to far beneath the surface of an ocean? But questions could wait, now he had to ensure that he survived.

He inflated his lungs, rearing high from the water, turning as he fell beneath the surface to rise again and look in a new direction. The circle complete, he rested again, conserving his strength, face grim as he stared at the vivid azure of the sky.

Nowhere had he seen a sign of land. On all sides stretched the empty expanse of the ocean, the surface broken by a gentle swell beneath the impact of a minor breeze. Above the sun, at zenith, showed a mottled surface tinged with green, the corona prominent, ringing the orb like a fringed halo. A film of cloud hung like a mist, more, darker, low on the horizon.

He was completely lost, naked in an ocean beneath an unfamiliar sky.

He fought the instinct to turn, to strike out and swim away from where he was, to head toward a point on the horizon. Action without a plan would be useless, and to waste his strength now would be to invite death. Already he felt thirst, the sun and brine acting to rob his body of moisture, but he knew the feeling was more a prelude to what would come than actually real. Real thirst would come later, together with hunger and fatigue. He could do without food for a while; the Cluny Discipline of which he was a master would enable him to control his metabolism to abrogate the need of sleep for days if necessary; thirst also could be controlled. But there were other dangers.

He caught the glimpse of a fin to one side, a wickedly pointed triangle that sliced through the water, vanishing to reappear a little closer, circling to vanish again. A predator, perhaps, scenting prey, cautious as yet but curious. And where there was one there would be others. The rule of the jungle held at sea as well as on land. Kill or be killed. Eat or be eaten. The basic law of survival.

Kennedy moved, threshing, slapping his palms hard on the water, hoping to scare the creature away. Naked and unarmed he was too vulnerable in an environment the beast had made its own. Even if he killed it, its blood would attract more of its kind and he would have no chance against more than one.

66

He reared again, eyes narrowed, searching, this time the immediate area. A dull patch showed on the swell a few hundred yards to his right. He reared again, catching in the moment before he fell an impression of solidity. As he fell back into the water he struck out for it, muscles rippling beneath his skin as he glided through the water.

Luck was with him. The thing was a tree, the bole knotted and scarred, the branches thick with decaying lichen, the wood soaked, waterlogged, barely able to float. It sank as he climbed on the trunk, rising slowly beneath his feet, offering a long, narrow refuge from the ocean. It was, he saw, about twenty feet long, one end fringed with roots, the other jagged with scaled branches. A tree which had grown close to a shore, to finally yield to the impact of waves during a storm, to drift and float beneath the vagaries of wind and current.

Kneeling, Kennedy dug his fingers into the knotted bark, pulling away rotten segments. The wood was pulpy, soft, and with a coarse grain. Such a tree would quickly absorb water and quickly sink. The land from which it had come could not be far.

An island, perhaps. The ocean could be dotted with them, small atolls bearing a few trees grown from windblown seeds and little else. But, compared to the empty expanse of the sea, such an island would be a haven.

He looked in the direction of the soft wind. Air, heated by the sun and rising from the warmer mass of land, would create such a wind. If the current was not against him, the rough craft he rode could eventually be carried to shore. If it didn't sink first. If no storm arose. If this world followed a familiar pattern. And, he thought grimly, if he could survive that long.

The tree rocked a little beneath his feet. He moved, balancing, only to feel the movement accentuated. Some of the branches dipped beneath the waves, others, rising, dripped water from dangling tendrils of slimed weed. From the sunken branches something rose, questing. A long, thin appendage covered with suckers and fringed with hooked spines. A dull patch could have been a rudimentary eye. Kennedy watched it, muscles tense, body poised for action.

He was not alone.

He backed a little as it came into view, humping, other tentacles joining the first, the suckers gripping as it moved its weight. The body was five feet long, a mass of tentacles sprouting from around a gaping mouth, the sac tipped by a whiplike tail spiked with a vicious horn. The mass was armored with overlapping plates. He could see no signs of limbs or appendages other than the tentacles and tail.

A sea-beast, he decided, one which had found a lair among the branches, lurking deep as it waited for prey. And now it was challenging that thing which had occupied its territory – or was seeking an easy meal. It made no difference. Kennedy was trapped with it on the only solid material in an empty ocean. Only one could survive.

He retreated back to the tangle of roots as the creature advanced, water lapping over the bole as it sank beneath the added weight. It was slow, out of its element, and there was something mechanical in its relentless determination. The plates of its armor showed dull as they dried beneath the sun, the tentacles had a rubbery appearance. The sound of its breathing was a gusting sigh.

Kennedy watched as the tentacles reached toward him, judging time and distance, his mind a coldly calculating machine of destruction. Around the tree he could see the wicked fins, a group of them now, endlessly circling. Behind him the root barred further retreat. In a matter of minutes he would have to fight for his life, and the odds were against him. Bare-handed he would have little chance against the hooked spines, the horned tail, the teeth he could now see in the gaping jaws. Even if he managed to kill the beast, he would be badly injured and death only delayed. And, if during the fight he should fall or be thrown into the sea, the circling predators would finish the job.

He tensed, bunching his muscles and as a tendril lashed at his eyes, he dived.

He hit the water clean, leaving barely a ripple, arching his back to skim just beneath the surface, strong arms sweeping forward and back to gain speed, reaching out to grip the branches ahead. He clamped his hands on a scaled limb and rose from the water as something darted toward him, triangular fin like a knife as it cut the ocean. Kennedy ignored it, watching the beast at the far end of the bole. It had paused, tentacle weaving, the dull patches of its eyes turning in his direction. If he remained utterly immobile his presence would not register but that was impossible, and there was a better way.

He had already selected the branch. Now he rammed his bare foot hard against the bole as he gripped it with both hands

It was thick, the scales rough, slimed with lichen. It bent a little as he heaved. He tried again, turning his body into a spring, concentrating his strength on arms, shoulders, and back, ridges of muscle showing along his thighs, his calves hard as if sculptured from stone.

The branch bent again, then broke free of the bole with a ripping tear. The upper section was thin, rotten with absorbed water. Kennedy broke it short across his knee, leaving a crude, clublike spear, one end massive, the other splintered into a sharply jagged end. Quickly, before the beast could turn, he ran toward it.

Waiting would have been an advantage. The sun was drying out the plates of armor and would create discomfort to a thing used to the cool depths, but he dared not wait. A slip, a misjudgement, and the battle would be over. He had to kill it before it could turn and bring its tentacles to bear. Around him the waiting fins made a second dive a gamble with death.

The tail lifted as he advanced, the cruel horn at its tip swinging down. He dodged it, but felt a touch on his thigh, saw the skin part as though slit with a knife, and a rill of blood oozed from the wound. As the tail lifted to strike again, he slammed at it with the thick end of the branch, driving it through the air with all the power of back and shoulders. It hit with a soggy impact, smashing the tail to one side, shattering to leave him holding only a couple of feet of jagged stick.

Immediately he sprang to land on the body of the creature.

Tentacles swept up, reaching backward, unable to extend to where he crouched. The tail twitched, lifted sluggishly, then fell to rise again. The jarred nerves had been bruised, the appendage momentarily numbed, but he knew that the damages he had inflicted were slight. He had gained a temporary advantage, that was all. His life depended on making it pay.

Savagely he dug the fingers of his left hand beneath one of the overlapping plates of armor.

He pulled, jerked, thrust the stick between his teeth, and sent his right hand to join the left. Drawing up his knees, he used his thighs to gain leverage and hauled upward at the plate. Something ripped and a gush of thin, yellow ichor wet his hands. The plate lifted, scraps of tissue hanging from beneath, exposing the raw flesh from which it had been torn. Quickly Kennedy snatched the jagged stick from his mouth, and lifting it high, drove it deep into the body like a knife.

The body heaved.

Kennedy was flung upward and back. He felt himself falling turned in the air to grasp a branch, and lifted himself up as his body hit the water. Something rasped beneath his heel and the tree quivered as to the impact of a heavy body beneath the mesh of branches. It moved again as the injured creature turned tentacles lifted, air gusting from the open mouth.

It was hurt, shocked, out of its familiar environment. I wanted to return to its lair, kill the thing that had attacked it eat so it could breed. Instinct guided the rudimentary brain. I moved, yellow ichor spouting from around the jagged stick turning into a flood as a tentacle jerked it loose.

Kennedy threw his weight against the branches on which he had climbed. He waited his moment until the rocking tree had turned to its full extent, accentuating the movement so that the yellow ichor stained the water which lapped high against the side of the beast.

His allies were waiting.

Before the bole could swing back, they attacked, fins slicing the surface, heads lifting, jaws wide to show rows of savage teeth. Tentacles threshed as those jaws closed over the armored body, the spined tail, ripping free chunks of flesh, pulling the creature from the bole into the ocean, where it threshed in violent death.

Kennedy waited, riding high, watching as the turmoil ceased and the fins, momentarily satiated, resumed their patient circling. The tree rode higher now, offering maybe a foot of height above the water. A tiny refuge a few feet long and a few inches wide, but it was all he had and it would have to serve.

Until he reached land. Or died of starvation or thirst. Or until the storm clouds thickening on the horizon came close to whip the sea into raging turmoil, and wind or waves washed him from his perch.

CHAPTER NINE

Saratov said sharply, 'Jarl! Look!'

'What is it?' Luden had been deep in thought, almost dozing as he let his mind toy with a thousand abstractions and possibilities, using the method he had so often before used with success when faced with an apparently insoluble problem. Now he rose from his chair and crossed to where the giant stood beside the couch. 'Penza?'

Kennedy had been stripped, the firm, hard lines of his well-proportioned body clear in the light of glowing lanterns. His skin shone with the oil Saratov had worked into his muscles, marred now with a thin, red line.

'There!' Saratov pointed at it. 'It suddenly appeared, Jarl. One moment there was nothing, the next there it was.'

'A shallow scratch.' Luden was annoyed. 'You should be more careful, Penza. You must have caught him with a nail.'

'How?' The giant lifted his hand. His nails were clipped, filed round and smooth to the tips of his blunt fingers. 'Anyway, Jarl, I was working on his other leg. And what about that?' He pointed to a graze beneath the left heel. That wasn't there before either.'

Luden pursed his lips as he examined it. Without comment he took a magnifying glass from the bag of supplies Chemile had brought and stared intently at both wounds.

'My apologies, Penza; you were not to blame. The heel seems to have been scraped by something rough, like a file. The thigh shows signs of tearing and bruising as if struck with something hard and sharp. A relatively dull knife swung with

71

tremendous force and barely missing. But how? You did not cause the wounds, so how could they have been made?'

Another question and one for which there was no immediate answer. Information, thought Luden. He could do nothing without it. None of them could. They must have facts, incontrovertible data, the foundations on which to build a plan to restore Cap to normal. If he could be restored . . . but Luden refused to think of the alternative.

Saratov said, 'Veem's taking his time. Do you think I should look for him? He might be in trouble.'

'He'll be back when he's learned something.' Luden turned as a knock sounded at the door. 'This could be him now.'

But it was the serving girl they had met before, the one who had been paid to spy. She was nervous, ill at ease, yet driven by some motive Luden as yet did not understand. As he opened the door, she held out her hand. In it was a charm bearing a symbol which was a copy of the one she wore around her neck. The Zheltyana Seal, the universal sign of good fortune.

She said, 'I heard. Your lord is ill. Is it your pleasure that I give him this gift?'

It was a charm bought from some vendor, a scrap of metal scratched with lines and over which an incantation had been mumbled, but Luden was touched. The girl knew no better and was doing what she could. To refuse would have been ungracious.

Gesturing her to enter the chamber, he said, 'You are more than kind. I must give you something in return.'

'No!'

He frowned at her abrupt refusal, and then understood. Good luck could not be purchased, only given. Unwittingly he had offended her sense of propriety.

'What is your name, girl?'

'Ulna, my lord. Of the House of Chem. Bonded to the palace and the service of the Lord of Jarhen.' Her eyes strayed to the couch on which, covered with a blanket now, Kennedy lay. 'He will live?'

'Yes.'

'And be well?'

'Perhaps.' Luden could never bring himself to believe in omens, but, at times, chance took peculiar forms. 'How long have you worked in the palace?'

'Many years, my lord.'

72

'And you know it well?'

'Of course, my lord.' She was puzzled. 'Why do you ask?'

Deliberately he said, 'You know where the treasure is hidden? The place where the Jewel is kept?' He read the answer in her eyes. 'Will you tell me? Draw me a plan?'

It was too much to ask her to act as guide. Quickly he added, 'There are guards, no doubt? Strong doors and many locks?'

'Even so, my lord.' Again her eyes drifted to where Kennedy lay. 'May I place the charm around his neck?'

Saratov stepped close as Luden nodded and, as the girl stooped over the supine figure, rumbled in a whisper, 'What's on your mind, Jarl? Has the Jewel something to do with what happened to Cap?'

'That is obvious, Penza. I would like to examine it more closely. Unfortunately, we shall not be given official permission. However, the girl seems entranced by Cap and may be willing to help.'

'She could report us,' reminded the giant. 'I've the feeling we won't be welcome if they think we're after the Jewel.'

'True, but that is a risk we must take.' Luden spoke louder as the girl turned toward him. 'Your charm will help, my dear, but other things might be necessary. If you help, you will not have cause to regret it.'

She made no answer, stepping toward the partly open door, lamplight golden on her skin, bright on the gold which tipped her fingers, her toes, the nipples of her breasts. Her face was drawn, thoughtful, the eyes veiled, and Luden wondered if she had come as a spy, bribed by Rem Naryan to learn what she could find.

And yet he doubted it. The Chambodian knew that he had won, that Jarhen would join his Complex, and now, to him, Kennedy would be of no importance.

A portion of the wall moved as the door closed behind her and Chemile came into view. He looked tired, his eyes red, his shoulders slumped so that he seemed to have shriveled a little, his normal, boucing ego numbed by what had happened.

He said, 'Cap?'

'The same.'

'I'd hoped – ' He shook his head. 'You took a chance there, Jarl, and it was unnecessary. I could have found out where the treasure is kept given time.'

'Time we may not have, Veem. It was a calculated risk. The girl is obviously attracted to Cap and may be willing to help. In any case the harm, if harm it is, has been done.'

'Even so –'

'Shut up, Veem,' rumbled Saratov. 'Jarl did what he thought best, and it's no good arguing about it. What have you learned?'

'Nothing helpful. The Chambodians are locked in tight. They seem to be having some form of celebration and are very pleased with themselves. I managed to get into the Inchonian quarters. Thom Ochran is dead.' He paused, then added meaningfully, 'Drowned.'

'Drowned?' Saratov frowned. 'Are you sure, Veem? We saw him fall; he was nowhere near water. How the hell could he have drowned?'

'That's what is puzzling his aides. I heard them talking. His lungs and stomach were full of brine. You were too busy to notice, but it spilled out of his mouth when they picked him up.'

Dead, as Hilton had died; but if one, why not the other? How had Cap escaped? Luden frowned, thinking, recalling the moment when the Jewel had pulsed. Kennedy had been intently concentrating on the thing in the box, the Inchonian too, and Rem Naryan had been as close. How had he remained unaffected?

He said, 'Pena! Just before Cap fell, what were you doing?'

'Looking.'

'At the three delegates?'

'Them and others.' Penza told what he had seen. 'I had the impression that Rem Naryan wasn't looking as hard as the others. In fact, his head was lifted a little as if he looked beyond.'

'That's the impression I gained,' said Luden. 'I was a little before them, turned to one side, and I think his eyes were closed. His aides, certainly, showed no interest. It was almost as if they were engaged on some enterprise or had been given orders of some kind. And I know that he knew about the Jewel. He'd asked Denog Wilde about it and suggested that it be used. It's almost as if he wanted it produced to solve the impasse, and that is strange if he was aware of its method of operation. A lie detector would have shown that he misrepresented the truth – the surest way to ruin his hope of an alliance.'

Chemile stirred. 'You think he set it up, Jarl? That it was a trap of some kind?'

74

'The possibility cannot be ignored, even though, at present, I cannot begin to understand the mode of operation. Think of the Jewel as a bomb,' Luden explained. 'Even if you had a method of triggering it, how could you be certain to avoid injury? Rem Naryan, as we know, stood very close. True, he didn't appear to be concentrating as hard as the others and may even have had his eyes closed at the time, but the effulgence was of a psychic, not a physical, nature. Closed eyes would have given no protection or very little. Yet, if he engineered the pulse, he must have been certain that he would not be affected.'

'We could find out,' suggested Saratov. 'If I could get my hands on that vulture he'd chirp all he knows.'

'I doubt it, Penza, and this isn't the time for the use of force. Later, perhaps, but not now. Our immediate problem is how to bring back Cap.' Automatically Luden glanced toward the couch. The charm the girl had left shone with a metallic luster in the soft light. A foolishness, but he had been equally foolish in asking the albino for his aid. Spells and incantations, ancient symbols, and moldering skulls would not provide the answer. Science alone could do that. 'Penza, where is the stone found on Hiton's body?'

'Here.' The giant passed it over. 'You think there might be a connection, Jarl?'

'Both Hiton and Thom Ochran died of drowning. That must be more than a coincidence. A gem is involved with both cases, the Jewel of Jarhen and this.' He tossed the stone, catching it, looking at the dull surface, the yellow substance. 'You saw the Jewel, Penza. Would you say there is a similarity?'

It was hard to tell. A diamond was crystallized carbon, the same substance as soot, yet though alike the appearance was totally different. And many-faceted stones bore a superficial resemblance to each other. The Jewel had blazed with light, but the one Luden held was dull, and he had caught only a glimpse of the object within the box.

He said slowly, 'I can't be sure, Jarl, but, at a guess, I would say there is.'

'Is that how Hiton died?' Chemile took the stone and examined it. 'This planted where he would find it and then triggered off? But how would that fill his lungs with water? How can a gem cause a man to drown? It doesn't make sense.'

'It happened, Veem.' Luden was sharp. 'Penza and I actually saw it. The Jewel must be the cause, there is no other logical

75

explanation, and this stone could be of the same material. In any case there is a connection, and one we must investigate.' He glanced at the giant. 'Is something wrong, Penza?'

Saratov took his hand from his pocket. Dangling from his blunt fingers was the ornament he had bought in the square. The lamplight caught the fine wires, the stones connected to them in an irregular pattern. Without speaking he took the gem from Chemile's hand and compared it to the others.

'Lamilite,' he whispered. 'The dexter form. I didn't think – I never guessed.'

Luden caught Chemile by the arm, restraining his impatience.

'I remember now,' continued Saratov. 'As Cap leaned over the Jewel I had an uneasy feeling. I tried to warn him; you remember, Jarl? You paid no attention. And then, when the Chambodian joined the others, it returned. I had my hand in my pocket and must have squeezed these stones.'

Chemile was curt. 'So?'

'The dexter form of lamilite is piezoelectric. Apply pressure and you get a current.' He lifted his eyes from the ornament. They were haunted. 'Can't you see what that means? You spoke of a trigger – I supplied it. It's my fault that Cap is how he is!'

CHAPTER TEN

The storm broke at dusk after a long day in which there had been nothing to do but wait. Kennedy had seen it coming, dark clouds rolling from the horizon to cover the sky, the rising wind lashing the water to foam. All he could do was to wedge himself among the branches as high above the water as he could get, hands clamped to the wood. The first blow had sent waves bursting over him, the wind rising to a scream, the surface of the ocean lashed to a frenzy. There had been only one consolation; in such weather the creatures which had tirelessly circled his precarious raft would go deep, seeking untroubled waters far below.

The rest had been nightmare. A time of holding on, of fighting to breathe, water like hammers pounding at his face and body, tearing at his grip and smashing the branches to which he clung until they had broken to be swept onward on the crest of a wave, himself more often submerged than afloat. Finally he was beached, more dead than alive.

He had crawled up a slope of sand, coughing water from his lungs, blind instinct driving him on and upward away from the surging waves, to fall at last beneath the shelter of a rock, there to slump in an uneasy state of semiconscious awareness as the night passed and the storm finally blew itself out the following noon.

He rose, ignoring the ache in his bones, the nag of overstrained muscles. He was tired and needed rest, food also, and his mouth was parched and caked with salt. He needed fresh water, food, and weapons. A fire, too, as a signal if nothing else.

If there were people here, he needed to find them, to answer questions if they could offer no other aid.

A clump of trees grew on the brow of a low hill, the branches torn, fruit littering the ground. It was hard, the skin tough, the pulp coarse and devoid of juice. He bit into one, sharp teeth shearing through the rind and mangling the pulp beneath. Unripe, the nutritional value would be small, but he was in no position to be selective. A stream lay beyond the hill and he bathed, washing salt from his body, rinsing his mouth, drinking sparingly. The sides of the stream were of rock and carried no traces of human or animal life. Kennedy picked up two stones, each as large as a closed fist, handy things with which to strike and convenient to throw should the need arise. Before dark he had to make a fire.

The wood of the fallen branches was soft and green, but finally he found a dead tree, the underside dry enough to be scraped for tinder. A strip of woven bark made a string, a thin branch a bow, two scraps of wood supports for the primitive drill. He placed one between his feet as he squatted, the other on the upper end of the stick around which he had wrapped the string. Moving the bow, he spun the stick, the sharpened end set into the hollow he had gouged from the block between his feet.

It took a long time. A primitive would have done it faster, but he was the product of a civilization that spanned a galaxy of stars; a man used to controlling energies which would destroy worlds, now reduced to squatting naked on a stone, making fire from primitive implements.

The block smoked at last, a thin coil coming from a tiny point of smoldering tinder, growing as he carefully fed it with shredded fragments, springing to flame to lick at thicker portions. When he finally arose he had a fire that threw a small patch of radiance in the growing dusk.

When it was large enough he left, returning to the bank of the stream where it widened into rippling shallows. There had been no signs of life, but that meant nothing. Nocturnal creatures would only emerge at night and, in the heat and after the storm, they would be eager to drink.

In the starlight he waited, as immobile as a rock, a stone in each hand ready to throw. Waiting, he looked at the stars.

They lay thick on the heavens, points of shining radiance, curtains of luminosity holding winking colors. A dull patch spread like a stain, a cloud of interstellar dust hiding the light of the suns beyond. He had seen that sky before, when leaving the *Mordain*. At least he was still on Jarhen, or a world very close. It was comforting to know that Luden, Saratov, and Chemile were somewhere close.

And, waiting, there was time for thought. He thought of the Jewel, which had appeared to explode into light; the abrupt transition into the ocean where any other man would have died. Hiton, perhaps? But how could Hiton have been plunged into the sea? How could it have happened to himself?

He tensed as a shadow broke the line of water and stone. It squealed as his first stone smashed the spine, the squealing dying as his second, swung this time, not thrown, crushed its head. The beast was small, scaled, a lizard as large as a Terrestrial cat. Smashing one stone against another he produced a sharp edge, sufficient to cut the skin and spill the entrails. Washing the body in the stream, he skinned it and took a mouthful of the raw flesh. Raw meat supplied more energy; the fire was not for cooking.

An hour later he had a second beast, furred this time, with a mouth full of savage teeth. Returning to the fire, he skinned it, thrusting a stick through the uncleaned body and setting it over the built-up flames. The scent of roasting meat rose to mingle with the smoke, the smell of burning. Light and the scent of food, a good combination. Bait to attract any who might be in the vicinity. It was better than searching through the starlight over unfamiliar ground for a settlement which might not exist.

Withdrawing, he found his place between sheltering rocks and waited.

The fire died, to become a bed of glowing ash coated with a dull film, the animal suspended above charred and more a cinder than edible flesh. A gusting wind rose from the sea, the aftermath of the storm, causing sparks to fly from the embers and drift high in the air, tiny points of red and orange dancing as they faded. Beyond the revived glow of the coals something stirred.

Kennedy watched, not moving, as still as the rocks between which he crouched. The movement came again, a shifting of darkness on darkness, more sensed than actually seen, and then, abruptly, a man stood before the fire, hands snatching at the charred meat.

As he bit into the flesh Kennedy was on him.

79

A blow and he was down, nerves stunned by the skillfully applied chop to the side of the neck with the edge of a stiffened hand. Temporarily paralyzed he could do no harm. Quickly Kennedy scouted the area, searching for any companion to the fallen man, but he had been alone. Returning to the fire, he fed it with scraps of wood and, in the leaping flames, stared at what he had found.

A man as naked as himself, long hair matted from a sloping brow, the jaw prominent, the eyes small, deep-set beneath beetling brows. Dirt marred the skin, which was covered with bruises and abrasions, blood matted on a sparse coating of hair. The hands were spatulate, the nails thick and jagged. The nose was flat and broad. Between the parted lips could be seen strong white teeth, the canines prominent.

He stirred as Kennedy massaged the nerves and muscles of his neck, twisting his head, eyes wide with terror.

'It's all right,' soothed Kennedy. 'I'm not going to hurt you. Here.' He handed the man the cooked animal. 'Eat. It's yours.'

Slowly the creature sat upright. Saliva dribbled from his mouth as he looked at the food, hunger fighting his terror and winning. Eyes furtive, he bit and swallowed, barely chewing the meat, eating like a dog.

A dog, thought Kennedy, or a man so primitive that he hadn't yet learned the use of clothing or weapons. And, like all aborigines, he was thin, ribs stark against his chest, muscles stringy, his body devoid of fat.

He said quietly, 'What is your name?'

The man continued to eat.

'Who are you?' Kennedy sharpened his voice. 'Where is your village?'

The mouth opened and from the throat came a series of grunts. As Kennedy stared, the man pointed at the remains of the meat, at himself, then at the meat again.

'You want more? Then why don't you catch it?' He met the blank stare. An idiot, perhaps? The man had a tongue, so he could speak if he wished – or if he knew how. Patiently Kennedy said, 'Are you alone? Can you understand? Are you alone?'

Finishing the meat, the man looked at him. He smelled of sweat and rancid grease, urine and accumulated dirt. The long hair hanging lank over his face gave him the appearance of a wild animal, but the eyes showed glimmers of intelligence.

Pointing at the fire, he made a cupping gesture with his hands, moving them from above the embers to a point behind where he sat.

'The fire,' said Kennedy, understanding. 'You want it?' He thrust a stick into the flames and, when it had caught alight, handed it to the man. 'Here.'

The man snatched it as he had the meat. As he rose, Kennedy caught his arm, strong fingers sinking into the flesh to clamp on the nerves beneath.

'You want to go back home? Is that it?'

This time the stream of gutturals carried a note of urgency. The man strained against the restraining hand, but made no effort to use the torch as a weapon. Kennedy pointed to it, then at the sky. Twice he repeated the gesture.

'At dawn,' he said. 'When we can see where we're going. We'll leave at dawn.'

They walked in single file, the primitive leading the way, his torch held high, a bundle of sticks beneath his arm to provide replacements. Kennedy followed, carrying the fire-drill in one hand, a heavy stone in the other. After a while he stopped and made crude sandals for his feet from thick leaves and bark held with woven strands of a thin creeper. The man waited, watching, his eyes alert. As Kennedy rose, he ran ahead, waving his torch, a thin stream of smoke rising from the burning wood.

The ground evened, became soft with dirt and loam, and Kennedy guessed that he had been washed ashore on a headland. A ridge fell to a shallow valley, and his companion ran ahead, shouting and waving his torch. By the side of a small stream stood a cluster of others.

All were naked, the women squat, broad-hipped, and with pendulous breasts, their hair as long and as lank as that of the men. All were emaciated. They milled like animals around the ashes of a dead fire, the flames, Kennedy guessed, quenched by the storm. As the fire-carrier arrived, they thronged about him, touching his arms, patting his back, leading him to the ashes, where he fed wood to the torch and so built up a fire. As the flames rose, they shouted, clapping their hands, the sound of their thick gutturals rising with the smoke.

Kennedy halted, watching, uneasy at what he saw. There were no huts or shelter of any kind and that was wrong. There were no signs of slaughtered game and no traces of cultivation. The trees around had been stripped of fruit, leaves, and bark,

81

and the trampled grass was soiled with excreta. Animals would not live like that, but these were not animals. And yet they were not wholly men. Even primitives would have built shelters and, if not nomads, would have raised crops. And there were no children.

He pressed through them and studied the river. It was full of fish; as he watched a silver shape leaped from the water to descend with a splash. A lizard darted from under a bush and he killed it with a thrown stone. A mollusk from the river bank supplied a sharp-edged shell and he used it to cut open the creature and clean the body. Rising from washing the flesh, he saw that he was surrounded by watching eyes.

They were in a wide circle, men and women, all intent on his every action. A man picked up a stone. Another followed his example and began to search the bushes. Two more flushed another lizard, and throwing their stones, missed. They stared at each other, then at Kennedy, their eyes baffled.

Deliberately he ate the raw meat.

For a moment no one moved, and then the area exploded into activity. Men and women rushed around, shouting, finding stones and hunting game. Their noise defeated their object, but they kept trying. A man, tottering on the edge, fell into the river to rise, spluttering, a mollusk in his hand. He smashed it with a stone and thrust the raw meat into his mouth. A fish, startled, leaped from the water to be hit by a lucky throw. A woman dived after it and stood in the shallows eating it, skin, flesh, bones, and all.

Learning, thought Kennedy blankly. They saw what he had done and followed his example. But how could they have survived without knowing how to capture and eat game? And if they were so primitive, how did they know about fire?

He studied them more intently. There were three dozen of them, men and women in equal numbers, and all of apparently the same age. A group without a recognizable language and apparently without the ability to survive. But how had they arrived here and from where?

He felt a tug at his arm. The man to whom he had given fire was pulling, gesturing with his free hand. Kennedy followed him as he led the way to a point farther down the valley. A cleared space stood surrounded by trees stripped of fruit and leaves. In the center stood an obelisk, a truncated pyramid four feet high, the edges sharp, the stone polished as if buffed with machines. On each surface, deeply engraved, was the Zheltyana Seal.

Kennedy stood staring at it for a long moment, his face bleak. Beside him the man was pointing, lifting his hand toward the sky, sweeping it down to point at Kennedy's chest, lifting it again. Over and over, a repetitive gesture unmistakable in its implications.

'No,' said Kennedy harshly. 'I didn't come from the sky. I'm not responsible for you being here.'

Others had done that, the incredibly ancient race which had left the obelisk marked with their seal. The Zheltyana, who had vanished from all known worlds aeons ago.

They had dumped the group on this world as they must have dumped other groups on a thousand more, as raw material to live or die as circumstances dictated. Given fire and, perhaps, implanted knowledge, and left to make the best of what they found. Snatched from their homes, their brains tampered with, memory erased – who could tell? But of one thing there could be no doubt.

Kennedy wasn't on the world he had known. If he was on Jarhen at all, it must be unguessed ages in the past. Somehow he had been transposed, not only from the audience chamber in the palace of Umed Khan, but to a point long before civilization had even begun.

CHAPTER ELEVEN

Stuart Seward said, 'Maybe I could help you. I've had some experience in electronics and I'm pretty good with my hands.'

'That won't be necessary.' Luden was tired and both voice and face reflected his fatigue. One was sharp, brittle, snappish with irritation, the other was drawn, the cheeks sunken, his thin lips tightly compressed into a near-invisible line. For hours he had worked in the laboratory of the *Mordain*, testing, checking, conducting a series of delicate experiments on both the jewel which had been found in Hiton's pocket and the ornament which Saratov had bought.

'Could I make you some coffee, then?' If Seward was annoyed, he didn't show it; diplomatic training had masked his face.

With an effort Luden mollified his tone. 'No, thank you. I have to get back to the palace. Penza will be anxious.'

Luden could have used him, but Saratov had insisted on staying with Kennedy. The giant was suffering from a sense of guilt. And, perhaps, it had been for the best for Saratov to stay behind. Disturbed, the giant could have made a trifling error where none could be allowed.

The aide said, 'I feel pretty useless cooped up in here. Is there nothing I can do?'

'You can make sure the Chambodian vessel does not leave,' said Luden flatly. 'Under no circumstances must Rem Naryan be permitted to depart before Cap gives the word.'

'How can he do that?' Seward looked blank. 'And how can I stop the ship leaving?'

'We are armed. Use force if you have to.'

'Force?' Trained in diplomacy, Seward hesitated at the use of naked violence. That was for the military, the soldiers of the MALACAs, and those who commanded them; the agents of Terran Control, and, more specifically, those who worked for FATE. 'The political repercussions – '

'To hell with political repercussions,' snapped Luden. 'Use your imagination. Stage an accident, regrettable but effective. You could be checking the Dione – one blast at this range and the Chambodian ship will be crippled. Just make certain that it doesn't leave.' As the aide still hesitated, he added, 'That is an order. Obey it!'

A hard man, thought Seward as he left, but they were all hard men, Chemile, Saratov, and especially Kennedy. And Weyburn's orders had been plain: to put himself at their disposal. Had he known they would risk outright war? As a diplomat he had to find some way to avoid any confrontation, but how else to cripple a vessel?

Thoughtfully he went to check the Dione, vaguely troubled at this close proximity to an instrument of war, missing the comfort of the chambers in which he normally waged his verbal battles.

In the palace Saratov was pacing the floor, eaten by anxiety, his sense of guilt. As Luden entered the chamber, Penza paused, turning, shoulders bunching a little as if he steeled himself for what he dreaded to hear.

'Relax, Penza. You are not to blame.'

'Are you sure, Jarl?'

'Positive. The stones are lamilite as you said, and they are piezoelectric, but the connections lacked insulation and the current generated was dissipated before it could be effective. I tested each stone alone and in combination with all others and achieved no more than a trace signal on the finest detectors in the *Mordain*.'

'Then it wasn't a communicator of some kind?'

'No. It could have been copied from one and probably was, but whoever made it saw only the pattern and had no conception of its real function. As an artifact it is very interesting and, when we have time, we must rebuild it to discover the function of the original. However, that must wait.'

As must everything until the main problem was solved.

Luden glanced at the couch on which Kennedy lay, knowing that Saratov would have told him had there been any change, yet unable to prevent the movement of his eyes.

'He's just the same.' The giant answered the unspoken question. 'Aside from two more marks on the feet. They appeared after you left, minor abrasions, as if he'd stepped on sharp stones. How the hell could it happen, Jarl?'

'I don't know,' said Luden slowly. 'But I'm beginning to guess. A theory, nothing more.'

'Tell me.'

'Later. Where is Veem?'

'Searching the palace. That girl didn't come back. I didn't think she would, and Veem is doing what he can.' Saratov paused, then added bitterly, 'The Chambodians are getting ready to leave.'

'So soon?' Luden frowned. He had been busy and time had a habit of slipping past when he was engaged on something that held his interest. 'They can't be leaving yet,' he decided. 'Probably they are just moving some of their gear. Rem Naryan can't go until the pact is signed, and that won't happen until the stated time. Umed Khan would be tempting fate to do otherwise.'

'He's slippery,' rumbled the giant. 'Maybe he's arranged an omen of some kind. You can't be sure of anything when you're dealing with a bunch of superstitious fools.'

'You could be right, Penza. I'd better pay a visit to Denog Wilde.'

'To bribe him, Jarl?'

'That and to ask him something. In a manner of speaking you could call it a professional consultation.'

The albino had been working. He sat at his table, eyes red, the dish before him empty. Instead of a human skull he now had a reptile's skull, the bone fretted and almost black with age. The symbols too, had altered, chalk lines tracing a pattern as fine and as complicated as lace.

He said, 'Has your lord returned?'

'No.'

'I tried. Five times have I tried, using all my skill, and yet always the thread of life stretches beyond the length of my sight.' Denog Wilde gestured toward the skull. 'Even this, old as it is, cannot lead my eyes, and I can obtain nothing of greater age.'

'A stone?' suggested Luden. 'The Jewel itself?'

'It's not of the substance of living creatures and will not serve.'

Well, at least the man had tried, and now was not the time to use threats. From his pockets Luden produced vials of assorted drugs. 'If a man has a high fever, give him this.' The tip of one thin finger rested on a container of antibiotics. 'Also, if he has wounds that will not heal, sores and spots on the skin, liquid in the lungs, and pain in the stomach. For you, this.' Again the finger tapped, this time on vials of hallucinogens. 'They will open doors in your mind, sharpen your awareness, and bring you close to the realization of destiny.' A lie, but to a seer who could tell what assurance they would bring? And they would certainly impress a client. 'And this.'

Luden rested a chronometer on the table, the dial calibrated to parts of a second, the sweep hand adjustable to make one revolution an hour, a minute, and a second. Stop buttons, colored hands, and perfect machining made it a jewel of its kind.

As Denog Wilde reached for it, Luden said gently, 'It would not be wise for Umed Khan to sign a pact before the auspicious hour. You agree?'

'Of course.'

'And perhaps that time could be delayed by a day? This instrument will enable you to determine the moment with greater accuracy.'

They looked at each other with perfect understanding.

'It shall be as you say,' agreed the albino. 'I wish that I could help your lord as easily.'

'You can answer questions.' Luden produced the stone found on Hiton. 'Have you seen this before or others like it?'

The thin hands tipped with nacre took the stone and held it close to the pink eyes. Silently Luden handed over a magnifier, better than any the man could possess.

'We call it hamenga,' said Denog Wilde after a moment. 'A little has been found in the Mountains of Leish. It has no great value, for it does not hold its fire. Contact with the skin renders it dull.'

'Can the fire be restored?'

'At great trouble, yes. Long rubbing with silken cloths will do it. Or it can be exposed to a storm, when if the lightning strikes close, it will resume its glow.'

'And if the correct musical note is struck nearby?'

'That also,' admitted the albino. 'But it is a matter of chance and, as I said, wearing it quickly makes it go dull.'

Luden said quietly, 'If you could find a piece large enough to make a ball the size of a clenched hand and could cut it with five hundred and sixty-seven facets, each of a different size and each with subtle alterations of the angles, you would have – what?'

'What you say cannot be done.' The albino lifted his head, his eyes shrewd. 'But if you could, you would have something very much like the Jewel of Jarhen.'

'Yes,' said Luden. 'That's just what I thought. It would be interesting to check.'

'The Jewel is held inviolate!'

'As you told me. Still, it is an intriguing thought.'

'It cannot be done!'

'No.'

'There are guards, spells of great power, malefic influences – '

'So I imagined.' Luden dismissed the notion with a wave of his hand. He had gained a little of the man's regard, but knew better than to think he had gained his trust. He said, 'Certain marks have appeared on the body of the Lord of Sergan. They were not there when he fell. Can your skill explain them?'

The albino touched the magnifier.

'Keep it,' said Luden. 'It's yours.' And then, for the first time during the interview, his voice hardened to betray some of his seething worry and impatience. 'If you know anything, tell me. Now!'

It was little, but it was verification of a kind. Luden correlated it as he walked through the passages leading to the quarters set aside for them, moving automatically, barely seeing the guards, the bizarre decorations. A voice yelled from down a corridor and he heard the sound of running feet. A guard, sweating, eyes wild, stared at him, pike lowered.

'Hold! Did you see it?'

'See what?'

'A thing. A creature of darkness. It came and it went and who knows what mischief it was making. Are you sure you saw nothing?'

'Nothing.' Luden moved the tip of the pike away from his

88

throat. 'Must I remind you that I am an honored guest of the Lord of Jarhen?'

'My lord!' The guard snapped upright, the pike at his side. 'Is it your wish that I escort you to your chamber?'

'Thank you, no,' said Luden dryly. 'I can find my own way. And that thing you thought you saw, could it have been a trick of the light?'

'No! I – ' The guard broke off, catching the hint. His captain was far from gentle with those who caused false alarms. 'Perhaps you are right, my lord,' he admitted. 'The flambeau guttered; it could have been that.'

It wasn't and Luden knew it. As he closed the door behind him, he said to Saratov, 'Has Veem returned yet?'

'He's just come in.' The giant nodded toward the bathroom. 'He's having a wash; he needed it.'

'You want me, Jarl?' Chemile entered the room, toweling himself down. 'Those passages are filthy,' he complained. 'And dark. Let me tell you what happened.'

'I know what happened,' said Luden. 'You almost got caught. If I hadn't talked the guard out of it, he would have raised the alarm.'

'So what? They wouldn't have found me.' Despite his anxiety for Kennedy, Chemile was boastful. 'I found a secret passage,' he explained. 'It was dark and full of dust, but I managed to follow it to where it came out close to what must be the treasure house. There were a lot of guards, anyway. I ducked back and must have taken a wrong turning. That guard turned as I was closing the panel and I ran.'

Saratov said, 'Why? If you're so good, why bother?'

'I was dirty; you saw me. Even my talent has its limitations.'

Smeared with dust and grime. Chemile would be clearly visible against any background in which he tried to blend. Normally Saratov would have made a lot of it, enjoying the minor victory in their usual, good-natured bickering, but now he had neither the patience nor the inclination to bandy words with Chemile.

'Jarl?'

'I gained us some time, Penza. A day, at least. Denog Wilde will cooperate to that extent. And we had a most interesting talk.'

'How could you waste time swapping chat with a crummy

magician?' Chemile was outraged. 'I thought you'd be hard at work trying to save Cap.'

'I was, Veem.'

'How? Casting spells and muttering a lot of gibberish? Damn it, Jarl, Penza's doing what he can and so am I. You have all the brains around here, or so you always claim; can't you put them to better use?'

Luden bridled, then restrained his anger. Chemile was under strain as they all were, his outburst was a form of release, nothing more. It was a measure of his own concern that he had reacted so strongly at the suggestion he did not care and had squandered his time.

'Shut up, Veem!' Saratov's voice was a threatening rumble. 'You know better than to accuse Jarl of not caring what happens to Cap.'

'Did I say that?'

'You implied it.'

'Then I'm sorry.' Volatile as ever, Chemile was quick to apologize. 'I didn't mean it; of course Jarl cares as much as we do. It's just that – Hell, Jarl, you know what I mean.'

'I know.'

'It's just that I figured you may have got yourself sidetracked. You know how you are when intrigued with a problem, and all this belief in fate and destiny and those charms and things.' Chemile wasn't improving matters and he knew it. 'Did you learn anything from Denog Wilde?'

'A little. The man is a true scientist in that he does his best to be honest with what he considers to be his field of operation. Also, he is genuinely convinced of his abilities. He is working from a false framework, of course, false, that is, from our own accepted nature of the universe, but even so his skill is remarkable.' Luden paused, remembering the dish and what he had seen there, or had been made to see. The qualification was important. 'From him I gained verification of what I am now almost certain must have happened to Cap.'

'Almost, Jarl?' Chemile sounded disappointed. 'Can't you be positive?'

'No, Veem. As yet I have only a theory, and before that theory can be accepted as fact it must be proved. As yet I am not sure how to do that, but proving the theory is of secondary importance at the moment. What is important is to restore Cap to normal life. Before I could attempt that I had to discover not only the mechanics of what had happened, but how they affected him.'

'And?'

'I could be wrong, Veem. If I am, it means that we have made no progress, but I have a glimmer of the answer.'

Saratov growled deep in his chest. At times Luden could be too cautious, too precise. He said, 'Damn it, Jarl, you're not lecturing a scientific body and having to look at every word. If you know, tell us.'

'Very well, Penza. As I said I could be wrong – but it is my firm belief that, at this moment, in fact ever since he fell before the Jewel, Cap has been in two places at once.'

CHAPTER TWELVE

For a moment there was silence, and then Saratov crossed the room on heavy feet to the couch and stripped off the blanket under which Kennedy lay. He stared down at the lax figure, noting that more blemishes had appeared on the body, a long scratch across the right side of the chest, another on the upper left arm, deeper and oozing blood.

'Two places at once,' he said. 'Here and – where?'

'I don't know,' admitted Luden. 'A long way either in space or time. But between this body we see and the one containing his mind there is a connection. In his own way Denog Wilde proved it – and there can be no arguing with what we see. Injuries where none could logically exist.'

'Another body,' said Chemile blankly. 'But how could that be?'

'Again, I don't know, Veem. I told you my theory had yet to be proved. I can guess, but I cannot be certain. Maybe I never shall. It is enough that we have something to work on, a possible answer to the problem of getting him back.' Luden's voice became detached, as if he were expounding a theory to a group of associates. 'The body, as we know, consists of three basic parts: the physical, which can be divided into the body and the brain, and something other than physical; the mind, the ego, the individual awareness which makes a man what he is. Now consider this and please bear in mind that I am using the wildest of analogies. If the mind is a separate entity, perhaps a product of the brain, but only in the sense that a child is the product of a woman, then, theoretically, it should be possible to move it to a different location. If so – and bearing in mind that the ego is the product of the brain and must contain all the knowledge stored in that brain, which, in turn, means the total knowledge of the body – it should be possible for the mind to recreate the location it left. In other words, to provide itself with a body identical in every way to the one in which it had previously resided.'

'Wait a minute, Jarl,' protested Saratov. 'That would mean actual, physical creation. A mind cannot do that without mechanical aid.'

'As far as we know that is true, Penza. But Cap would have had aid – the power of the Jewel. Somehow its psychic resonance must have done three things simultaneously: it divorced Cap's mind from his brain, it sent it somewhere, and based on the pattern in his mind, provided energy to literally recreate his body. However, fortunately for us, the divorce was not total. A link remains. What happens to Cap's new body is reflected in the one he left behind. The blemishes are caused by actual wounds he has received in his new environment.'

Chemile said quickly, 'That means if he should be seriously hurt or killed wherever he is, this body here will show it. Even die?'

'Yes, Veem, and as we have no idea as to the dangers he is facing, we must recall him as soon as possible. That is why we need the Jewel.'

Luden produced the stone he had shown Denog Wilde from one pocket, a small case from another. With tongs, he touched the stone to a connection and, immediately, it shone with a golden luminescence.

'On this world they call it hamenga,' he murmured. 'A form of lamilite as you said, Penza, but not a true dexter form. There is a peculiar distortion in the shape of the crystals that makes it unique. Almost as if certain of the facets extended into another dimension. However, it can be stimulated either by electricity or harmonic resonance. I am using the latter method for greater control.' Carefully he placed the glowing gem on a table. 'Look at it,' he ordered. 'Not directly, but in a mirror. And just watch it without too much concentration. Look at it and think of something else. Now!'

He touched a switch. The stone pulsed and became dull again.

'The trigger!' Saratov stooped over the dull fragment. 'The

charge is unstable,' he muttered. 'A harmonic note causes it to dissipate. But the Jewel didn't go dull.'

'In comparison this thing is crude,' said Luden. 'A natural product containing flaws. The Jewel itself is probably synthetic and most carefully machined to rigid specifications.'

'You warned us against concentrating on it, Jarl,' said Chemile. 'Why? A psychic connection?'

'Yes, Veem. If my theory is correct, the very act of concentrating establishes a connection between the mind and the mechanism of the stone. Hiton would have been intrigued. Thom Ochran was engrossed, and we know how Cap will concentrate on anything which holds his interest.'

'So all Rem Naryan had to do was to look away, let his mind wander.' Saratov was grim. 'Well, that proves it; let's pay him a visit.'

'No, Penza.'

'Why the hell not, Jarl? You've just shown how it was done. It's time we got hold of that murdering vulture and make him bring Cap back to us.'

'I doubt if he knows how,' said Luden. 'I believe the Chambodians have stumbled on something they barely understand. They probably want this world so they can exploit the source of hamenga; it could turn out to be as valuable as chombite. But knowing that doesn't help us. And if we raid their quarters, we will lose all chance of getting the Jewel. Umed Khan will have us thrown from the palace.'

'Not for long,' said Chemile. 'I could get back in any time I wanted.'

'One man, Veem; the odds are too great against the possibility of success. And it would not be wise to move Cap – there is a relationship between the Jewel and this palace which could be of the utmost importance.'

Saratov had been thinking. He said, 'Couldn't we use this stone to bring Cap back?'

'Perhaps – if I knew more about its function. We are on the edge of a totally new branch of science, Penza, and one mistake could cost Cap his life. I am certain there must be a relationship established between him and the Jewel. We must get it at all costs. Without it, we could lose Cap forever.'

They would watch helplessly as his body showed more and greater injuries, telling of the tribulations he would be suffering, the dangers he would face. And there was more. The thin ghost-thread that alone connected the real and surrogate bodies could snap at any moment, and when it did, all hope would be lost.

'The girl,' he said. 'Ulna. Summon her here.'

'We don't need her.' Veem was overconfident of his skill. 'I can find the way to the treasure house.'

'We haven't the time for you to prowl around,' rumbled Saratov. 'What if you were seen again? Caught? We can't take the chance.' A gong throbbed beneath the impact of his fist. 'We'll do as Jarl says.'

She looked as she had before, tall, skin silken in the golden light, gold flashing, the strands of her skirt parting over rounded thighs. As she bowed the charm swung from between her breasts, the Zheltyana Seal dark against the metal polished by continual wear.

'My lord?'

Luden took her by the hand and led her to the couch. He said, 'The Lord of Sergan is dying. Only you can save him.'

'How, my lord?'

'He needs a spell of great power. The Jewel can provide it, but he has no means to find his way to where it lies. You could show him that way so that his spirit, lost now, may return. Can you draw?'

'Lines on paper, my lord?'

'Yes.' He led her to the table where Saratov had placed paper and a stylus. Quickly he drew familiar passages and rooms, resting the point of the stylus on the chamber in which they stood. 'We are here, you understand? Take this pen and trace the way to where the Jewel lies hidden.'

'A rune?' She looked at it, frowning. 'Will it aid your lord?'

'Only if drawn by your hand.' Luden produced a clean sheet of paper. 'Now, girl. Quickly!'

The plan was rough, corridors and chambers completely out of proportion, the finished item more like the mystic rune she thought it was than a useful map. But it was the best they could get and it would have to serve. Chemile studied it, frowning as Saratov ushered the girl from the chamber.

Returning, he said, 'Can you follow it, Veem?'

'Yes. No wonder I missed it. The treasure house lies at a lower level behind a false wall. That passage I found must lead close to where it lies. They'll have it well-guarded, though, and there'll be locks and bars.'

'I can take care of the guards,' rumbled the giant. 'The locks too.'

He meant it and could do it, the tremendous strength of his body could smash all opposition, but such action would arouse immediate alarm and retaliation.

Luden said, 'We must be subtle. We shall need time to restore Cap. Is there any other way into the treasure house other than by the door, Veem?'

'Through the roof, Jarl?'

'Or a wall. Can we get close enough to force an entry?'

He waited as Chemile studied the map. Of them all he was best qualified to make a decision; his excursions had carried him where they had not gone.

'There could be a way,' said Chemile at last. 'That passage I found could run past this wall. But we'll need lights and tools to break in.'

They had Kells, Luden's wrist-laser, and Saratov's strength. That, together with an ornamented bar the giant wrenched from a bathroom fitting, would have to be enough.

At the door Saratov hesitated. 'Should we be leaving Cap unguarded?'

For answer Luden pointed his hand at the door. The metal of the lock fused, joined in a weld stronger than any bolt.

'Quickly, Veem,' he said. 'Lead the way.'

They had luck, the guard was absent, the corridor containing the secret panel unwatched. Chemile led the way inside a narrow passage heavy with the odor of dust. The glowing blue fluorescence from the Kells showed a wall of solid stone faced by another of yellow bricks. The roof was low and thick with webs.

'This way.' His voice echoed dully in the cramped width of the passage. 'Lower down we hit a branch. Take the right-hand corridor.'

'And this way?' Saratov gestured in the other direction.

'I don't know. There's a grille a little way down, locked. It could lead to our chambers.'

'The Jewel,' reminded Luden. 'We have no time for speculation.'

He walked behind Chemile, Saratov in the rear, holding a Kell high to paint the passage with light. The dust was thick,

96

marked only by the recent passage of Chemile's feet, becoming smooth as he led the way from his traveled path. Twice he paused at the murmur of voices from behind the yellow wall; a third time he moved aside a small panel and peered through.

'Guards,' he whispered as he closed the opening. 'A dozen of them at least and all armed to the teeth. We must be close.'

A short flight of steps broke the smoothness of the descending ramp. The passage branched again, the yellow wall becoming blocks of moldering stone so that they edged through a tunnel of dressed rock. A locked grille barred the way.

Luden examined it. 'Penza!'

The giant pushed past, set aside the Kell, and gripped the bars with his massive hands. He strained, muscles bulging beneath the fabric of his shirt, and with a harsh snap of broken metal, the grille swung wide. Fifty feet farther on Chemile halted.

'This must be it,' he said. 'If the map is right, that must be the wall of the treasure house.'

Luden examined it. It was made of neatly fitted blocks and at one time had been painted with bright colors, a scene from some legend, he decided, now stained and faded, blotched by patches of extruded crystals. It was the wall of what once might have been an audience chamber, blocked in as the palace was enlarged, flanked by the passage in which they stood.

Saratov probed at it with his bar. The neat joints made it impossible to gain a purchase. Luden raised his hand and sent the invisible beam of the laser against the joint, the stone flaking, the joint widening as he slowly moved his wrist.

'Right, Penza. Try now.'

Saratov rammed home the end of the bar and heaved. Cords stood out on his neck and throat, muscles becoming like iron as his feet thrust at the floor to gain purchase. The block shifted a little with a dry rasping and a thin rain of mortar came from the widening joint. He dug the bar deeper and heaved again. Like an opening door the block swung from its position. Saratov thrust it back, moved the bar to the far end, and resumed his leverage. Slowly the block crept from the wall.

It was a cube two feet on a side. He dragged it from the wall and attacked another, a third. Dust filled the passage, catching at their eyes and clogging their nostrils. In the light of the Kells they could see other blocks through the patch he had made.

'It must be an inner wall.' Saratov stooped, squinting. 'Not as thick, I hope. We're lucky they didn't bind them together with traverse blocks.' He probed with the bar. 'This one, I think.'

The metal made a dull rasping as he tore at the mortar. It rose to echo down the passage, to be answered with a faint scratching, a snapping as of metallic castanets.

'Penza, a moment!'

Luden stood, listening in the uneasy silence. The scratching came again, louder, as if something moved down the tunnel where it curved, dark beyond the light of the Kells.

Chemile whispered, 'What is it, Jarl?'

It was a guardian, set to watch the passage, contained by the locked grilles, lying dormant perhaps for decades, centuries, now woken by the noise they had made. It came with a flurry of limbs, exoskeleton dully ebon in the glow of the Kells, mandibles snapping with a horrible metallic hunger.

A thing like a wingless wasp, a beetle, as long as a man, it had serrated claws that could shear through an armored body.

Luden stepped forward to meet it. The charge in the wrist-laser might be low, the weapon undesigned to kill such a creature, and the massive body would take a lot of stopping, but he was determined to do what he could. As a claw lifted toward him he fired, smoke rising from the base of the appendage, ichor welling from the gaping wound. Again he fired, aiming for the eyes, twin saucers faceted like jewels. Blinded, the creature reared, foul odors gusting from the palpitating mouth, chiton rasping against the walls to either side.

'Jarl! Back!'

Saratov had picked up a block of stone. He stood, like a figure from legend, the great cube lifted high above his head. He threw it as a normal man would throw a rock. Powered by the incredible strength of his body it flew through the air to land with a soggy impact on the wicked head, crushing chiton, tissue, the ganglia beneath, to rest in a pool of noxious ichor.

'A good throw, Penza.' Chemile wiped at odorous moisture that had spattered his torso. 'Let's hope there aren't any more inside.'

Luden led the way, wriggling through the small opening Saratov dug from the wall, standing with a Kell in his hand as Chemile joined him. Thick doors barred one end of the chamber, which was long and narrow and filled with chests of a variety of sizes, all closed. Runes were painted on the walls, and a mesh of protective symbols covered the ceiling. The floor was of stone, hollowed in places, broken in one place by a trapdoor.

Chemile said thoughtfully, 'The Jewel of Jarhen is the most precious thing this world possesses – at least the rulers think so. Under that trap, Jarl?'

'Probably, but be careful, Veem. There could be protective devices.'

Some pikes stood against the wall, their shafts studded with precious gems, the blades heavily chased with gold. This was ceremonial gear used only on special occasions, safely stored until a time of need. Chemile took one and with the point lifted the door of the trap.

Beneath rested a pedestal on which stood the gemmed container Luden had seen before.

'That box, Veem. But be careful!'

Chemile nodded and extended the pike. As the point touched the lid of the box, something flashed from the side of the pit.

'Neat.' He examined the shaft of the pike. It had been sheared through, the head laying where it had fallen beside the pedestal. A reaching arm would have been cut as easily. 'Let's see if it happens again.'

'The pit has four sides, Veem,' said Luden. 'And a barbaric mind is logical.'

Logical enough to have used each of the four. Three times blades flashed from where they had been resting, powered by compressed springs. Only when further probings with a pike produced no results did Chemile dare to snatch up the box.

'Got it, Jarl! Let's get out of here!'

When they returned to their chamber Nava Sonega was waiting.

CHAPTER THIRTEEN

He was attended by a half dozen guards, picked men of the ruler's bodyguard, armed not with ceremonial pikes but with swords and squat-barreled carbines: primitive weapons throwing a solid missile, but effective enough to maim and kill.

He said, 'The door of your chambers seems to be locked.'

Luden was curt. 'It is.'

'And your companion?' The vizier's eyes moved from Luden to Saratov. 'Is he within?'

Chemile was twenty feet away, at the turn of the passage, rigid in a corner with the box containing the Jewel between his back and the wall. Sonega glanced directly at him, saw nothing but the familiar background, and returned his attention to the others.

'He is meditating,' said Luden. 'As you know, the Lord of Sergan is not himself. We are trying to restore him to health.'

'With medication and meditation,' murmured Sonega. 'With the help of Denog Wilde and, perhaps, with the aid of a mystic rune drawn for you by a serving girl. A rune showing where the Jewel is hidden. Is that not so?'

The girl had talked or had been put to the question; it made no difference. Nava Sonega would never have been able to maintain his position without the use of spies and informants.

He continued, in his dry, rustling voice: 'The girl has not been harmed. In fact, she is concerned that your master be made whole again. Where is what she drew?'

'Destroyed,' said Luden. 'Burned so that the wandering spirit of the one within could find the aid he needs.'

100

Sonega waved away the guards. When they were beyond earshot, he said, 'For a man of science your words are strange. I like it better when you treat me as equal to yourself. The girl drew a map and we both know it. You asked me about the Jewel before, as you asked Denog Wilde. I do not think you are a thief. What is your interest in the Jewel?'

'I am certain it could restore my friend to normal life.'

'Perhaps it could, the Jewel contains great power, but it is beyond your reach and will remain so.' The dry voice hardened. 'I give you warning. The Jewel is inviolate. Should you, or any, obtain it by the use of some magic, the fact that you are strangers on this world will not save you. The penalty is impalement. Not even Umed Khan could prevent it. On that matter tradition must not be broken.'

Saratov rumbled, 'Impaled?'

'You know what that means. The stake is in the great square. Be warned!'

The giant drew in his breath as the vizier and his guard moved off. 'He means it, Jarl. I wonder he didn't have us searched. He suspects something.'

'There was no reason for him to order a search.' Luden was precise. 'As far as he knows, the Jewel is safe in the treasure house. He came to warn us, that is all. But if Veem hadn't been so fast – '

'We'd be on our way to the stake now.' Saratov looked grim. 'A hell of a way to die. Do you think he will check? If he goes looking for that Jewel and finds it missing, all hell will break loose.'

'The probability that he will is high, Penza,' said Luden. 'And if he does, the situation will become difficult. He will certainly return to search. Before he does, we must rescue Cap.' He aimed the wrist-laser, but the weapon was exhausted. 'Penza, the door if you please.'

The weld broke beneath the thrust of the giant's boot, the panel flying open. As he closed it, Chemile slipped into the chamber.

'Here.' He held out the box. 'Take it, Jarl. It feels red-hot.'

It was a metaphor, but an apt one. The word was cool, the crusted gems like ice, but possession of it was enough to send them all to an agonizing death. As Saratov barred the door, Luden lifted the lid. Chemile drew in his breath as he saw the Jewel.

'It's beautiful. No wonder they guard it so close. I know a dozen worlds where it would bring a fortune.'

And a hundred more where it would be valued for its scientific interest alone. Luden touched it, the tips of his fingers caressing the surface, knowing that it held a secret which would open new doors to scientific advancement, willing to trade all but a year of his life to learn it. A year in which to solve questions which had tormented men through all of recorded history. The very answer to life itself, perhaps. To creation.

'Jarl!' Saratov was anxious. 'We'd best hurry.'

'Of course.' Luden became brisk. 'First I must determine the resonance that activates the pulse and then determine the exact corresponding modulation that will, for want of a better term, provide a negative to the original positive. We need to send a signal to the point in space and time where Cap's mind is now. A signal which will reverse the effects of the original impulse. I think it had best be tackled from a radiated harmonic – we lack equipment to make a thorough electronic and radio-active examination.'

'Wouldn't ultrahigh frequency give a sharp measure of control, Jarl?'

'It would, Penza, and I suspect the Chambodians used a radio-trigger. However, we do not simply want to activate the pulse, but modulate it. If my theory is correct, it is best done by using a narrow beam of focused ultrasonic waves.'

As Luden talked he was working, manipulating the instrument with which he had triggered the stone found on Hiton's body. As the Jewel flared in a gush of searing brilliance it glowed into life.

'A relationship,' said Chemile. 'The stone is picking up energy from the Jewel.'

'More than that, Veem. I think it is modulating the radiation. Now, if it could be used as a form of rectifier –'

Luden bent to work, reaching for his pocket computer, thin fingers dancing over the sensitized nodes. From time to time he made a test, checked his figures, added more symbols to a growing equation. Unable to help, Chemile wandered around the rooms, tapping the walls, listening.

Watching him, Saratov growled, 'What are you looking for? Secret passages?'

'We know they exist, and one might run from these rooms to

102

those of the Chambodians. They must have got that stone to Hiton in some way.'

'Sure, they just gave it to him.'

'And he took it? Would you? Hiton knew better than to trust those vultures. He might have accepted a gift because of the need of diplomatic tact, but he wouldn't have taken it to bed with him. My guess is that he found it lying beside the bed. Maybe he woke and saw it. It would be glowing and he would be curious. He would pick it up and stare at it, examining it, and then – ' Chemile snapped his fingers. 'Rem Naryan or one of his aides activated the trigger.'

'And they couldn't find it afterward,' mused Saratov. 'It had slipped into his pocket, and maybe they didn't have time to make a thorough search.'

'Which means it happened shortly before the aide brought in his tisane. Whoever did it couldn't have escaped through the door, so there must be a secret passage.' Chemile grunted. 'This could be it.'

A narrow panel had swung open beneath his fingers, revealing a corridor beyond. The dust on the floor was marked by footsteps.

'Penza! Let's – ' Chemile broke off as the sonorous throb of a gong vibrated the air. It was repeated, joined by the brazen clangor of beaten rods of brass, the wail of a horn. 'The alarm! They've found out the Jewel is missing!'

'And they'll come looking for it,' snapped the giant. 'Jarl!'

Luden could move fast when he had to. As Saratov spoke, he rose from his chair and crossed to where Kennedy lay. He had the box containing the Jewel in one hand, the stone found on Hiton's body resting on the lid. It glowed with brilliance.

'Open Cap's jaws, Penza. Clamp the stone between his teeth. Don't touch it with your bare hand, use the tongs.'

Feet ran past the chamber as the giant obeyed. From somewhere down the corridor came the harsh snap of orders, the words lost in the roar of the gong.

'Hurry,' urged Chemile. 'The vizier wasn't joking. If they find the Jewel, we'll all be impaled.'

Luden ignored the comment. 'Lift him up, Penza. I want him to stare at the Jewel.'

He raised the cover and held the open box so that the effulgence of the Jewel bathed the lax features, the strong fingers of the giant as they lifted the eyelids, the dull orbs beneath.

'A chance,' he said worriedly. 'We'll have time for only one attempt. I must activate the pulse before the stone loses its charge. If my calculations are correct, it will act as a modifier and send impulses via bone conduction direct to the brain.' He raised the instrument he had used to trigger the stone. 'Now!'

The Jewel pulsed.

A flood of radiance blazed from the open box, throwing Kennedy's face into stark detail, reflected from the opened eyes, rising to paint Soratov's features with lambent hues. Between the teeth the stone pushed in sympathy, fading a little as the effulgence died.

'Don't look at the Jewel, Penza!' Luden's voice was sharp. 'Nor you, Veem.' He made a slight adjustment on his instrument as a heavy knocking came from the door. 'Now!'

This time, as the radiance streamed from the box, he added his voice to the impulse.

'Cap! Come back, Cap! Return!'

Again the pulse.

'Cap! Answer! Return!'

Another adjustment and again the burst of effulgence, the snapped command. The knocking had increased and something heavy thudded against the panels. Within minutes, seconds even, the guards would burst into the chamber and all hope of rescuing Kennedy would be lost.

'Cap! Come back to us! We need you!'

With sudden desperation Luden made a final adjustment and, as the Jewel pulsed, activated the trigger of the stone. Kennedy stiffened, reared, his mouth opening, the stone falling as both hands lifted to grip the fingers holding his eyes.

'Cap!' Saratov's voice was a roar, rising above the pounding at the door. 'Cap! Stay with us!'

Kennedy turned, twisting, iron hands tearing away the giant's fingers. His eyes, no longer dull, looked at Luden, the box he held, the confines of the chamber.

'Jarl! And you, Penza. And Veem. I'm back, but how – '

Luden dropped the box and caught the reaching hands. Swallowing, he said, 'Are you all right, Cap? Is your mind clear?'

It was clear, but numbed a little by the abrupt shock of transition. Kennedy drew a deep breath, conscious of the noise, the harsh sound of splintering wood as the door smashed open. Instinctively he rose, body tensed as guards burst into the chamber. Nava Sonega was curt.

'The Jewel has been stolen. You will permit a search.' It was not a question. As the guards quested the rooms, he said, 'Why did you not open the door?'

'We were busy,' said Luden.

'With the Jewel?' Sonega stared at Kennedy. 'I see that your master has recovered his senses. I am glad to see it. Now, he, too, will take his place on the stake.'

'He will?' Saratov stepped forward, his big hands curved as if to grab, grip, and tear. 'Maybe you won't find that so easy.'

'Guards!' Nava Sonega spoke from behind the protection of aimed carbines. 'Attempt to resist and you will be shot. Broken knee-caps will render you helpless and save you for the stake. Where is the Jewel?'

Luden remained silent, wondering why it had not yet been discovered.

'You must have used it,' said the vizier. 'The Lord of Sergan is whole again and you insisted that it could only be done with the aid of the Jewel. If you did not take it, what did you use?'

'This,' said Kennedy. His mind was busy, extrapolating from presented data, filling in the parts he did not know. He held out his hand. On the palm rested the stone Luden had set between his teeth.

'That?' Sonega frowned. 'You used that?'

'I did.' Luden was curt. 'Now if you will leave, I can attend to the needs of my friend.'

A guard said, 'We have searched the chambers, my lord. The Jewel is not within.'

'Search again!'

The rooms, though spacious, were spartanly furnished. Guards delved into cabinets, the bag containing the items brought from the *Mordain*, the couch on which Kennedy had rested. Hands slapped at clothing, but Saratov stood immobile at Kennedy's sharp warning.

From where he leaned against a wall Chemile said, 'Satisfied? The Jewel isn't here. Maybe someone else took it.'

'It must be found,' said Sonega grimly. 'No one will be permitted to leave the palace until it is.' He felt baffled, giant strength had been needed to smash a way into the treasure house and to kill the guardian, and he had been certain the Jewel would be found in the quarters of the Terran delegation. Perhaps, by some means, they had hidden it; if so, there were

105

ways of discovering how. Denog Wilde with his skill would be able to discover where it was.

As the guards filed from the chamber, Sonega said, 'You will remain here. Food and wine will be sent to you. Guards will be outside with orders to shoot. Not until the Lord of Jarhen decides will you be permitted to leave.'

And that, thought Kennedy grimly, would not be until the Jewel was found. The strange stone that held the secret of an unsuspected science. He sat on the edge of the couch and tried to ease the turmoil of his mind. One second he had been sitting before the obelisk patiently teaching one of the group how to make fire. The woman had been clumsy, breaking the string of the bow, unable to control the spinning of the drill. He had mended the string and demonstrated how it should be done and had leaned back against the polished stone. The sun had been warm and he had looked up at it, pressing his head against the ancient sign.

One fragment of a second – and then he had been back in the chamber, feeling the clamp of hands around his head, the fire of the Jewel blazing in his mind.

'Cap?' Luden was anxious.

Kennedy straightened. 'I'm all right, Jarl. Fill me in.'

'It's over, Cap,' rumbled Saratov as Luden finished his terse explanation. 'The Chambodians have won. They'd have signed the pact now if it hadn't been for Jarl.' He scowled. 'When I think of what those damn vultures did! They shouldn't be allowed to get away with it!'

'They won't,' said Chemile. He had suddenly appeared, brushing flecks of dust from his lithe figure. 'If Denog Wilde is half as good as they say he is, those Chambodians are in for an unpleasant surprise.' He smiled, pleased with himself. 'I've dumped the Jewel in their quarters.'

CHAPTER FOURTEEN

The great hall was full of light, flambeaux, lanterns, search-beams culled from the houses around the square and set now to bathe the groined roof with colorful extravagance. Music rose, the heady throb of drums, the wail of pipes, and the nerve-tingling chords plucked from the strings of Quendish guitars. Serving girls hurried to and fro bearing trays laden with wine and cakes, fruits crusted with spices, comfits of rare and costly seeds bound with scented oils.

A feast worthy of the occasion, thought Umed Khan as he lounged in his chair of state. A celebration to acknowledge the immutable workings of fate that had guided the destiny of his world. And fate could not be denied. Portents were real and clear to a discerning eye. Omens guided the way and augurs were of value. Even the stars in their courses had fought for him.

From a passing serving girl he took a goblet of wine and sipped, brooding.

He had almost made a mistake. He admitted it and yet he had followed a path that was not to be. It was proof of the interest and power of destiny that it was not too late. A man had returned from the dead – what greater omen could there be? The Jewel had been lost and found again. And yet . . . ?

There no longer could be, he told himself firmly, any possibility of doubt. But he had felt this way before, only to have been proved wrong. If Denog Wilde had not stayed his hand, the pact with the Chambodians would have been signed by now. They knew it; why then should they have stolen the Jewel? And how could they have done it? Rem Naryan had been in audience, his aides attending him, and they could have no allies within the palace. And yet how could the Terrans be blamed when no evidence had been found of their guilt?

And yet the portents were clear. Troubled, he found refuge in the wine.

Watching Khan from where he sat at his place at the board Saratov rumbled, 'That man's in for a shock. Wait until MALACA Eight gets here and Commander Mbomoma gets to work. He won't know what has hit him. The deserts irrigated, the peasants fed, school to teach the futility of believing in lucky charms. It'll be a revolution.'

'A painless one,' said Luden. 'Mbomoma is a subtle man and knows how to handle superstition. He will replace old traditions, not destroy them.' He added, 'But we are anticipating, Penza. The pact has not yet been signed.'

'Can there be any doubt?' Chemile reached for a tray and helped himself to a cake. 'They found the Jewel in the Cambodian quarters – I'm surprised they haven't been impaled by now.'

'They've got an alibi,' rumbled Saratov. 'I heard a couple of the guards talking. They were with the ruler when the Jewel was stolen.'

'And they want this world,' reminded Luden. 'It holds much they consider of value.'

They wanted the lamilite, which they hoped would replace chombite – the mineral that fed the computers, each crystal holding an incredible amount of information, rare and precious gems culled from limited deposits. No wonder they had been eager to obtain an alternative. Kennedy's hand tightened on his goblet as he remembered what they had done. Ben Hiton, an old man, suddenly thrown into the depths of an ocean Thom Ochran too.

And himself hopelessly lost in time and space.

He leaned back in his chair, seeing again the pathetic group of men and women that had been dumped on a strange and hostile world. They had been like children, completely unaware of the dangers they faced, lacking the basic knowledge of survival. A beast had killed two of them before Kennedy had crushed its skull as a claw had raked his chest, a talon gouging his shoulder. And what if he had not rested his head against the obelisk at precisely the right time?

Luden was serious as he answered the question:

'I don't know, Cap, but I would guess that you would have stayed there. The artifact must have held a mechanism of some kind; a guide or a beacon which, in some way, responded to the pulse of the Jewel.' He added regretfully, 'It was a pity that you had no opportunity of taking careful note of the position of the stars. Any displacement would have given us a clue as to how far in the past you had been thrown.'

'I had other things to do,' said Kennedy dryly. 'And it seemed more important to teach those people to survive than to study the heavens. In any case we can't be sure I was in the past at all.'

'An alternate universe?' Luden chewed thoughtfully at a sweetmeat. 'That is a possibility I considered, but had no opportunity to determine. I am inclined to believe otherwise. If my theory is correct, the Jewel is actually a part of a device which was originally used as a means of rapid and efficient transportation. The recreation of the physical body could have been coupled with the total destruction of the initial location. In that case no connection would have been left. You would merely have entered the cabinet, assuming that one was used, concentrated on the desired point of arrival, and, immediately, you would have been there.'

'Matter transmission?'

'I think so, Cap. Divorced from its attendant mechanisms the Jewel acts as a wild variable. It sends the mind, but not totally, and it is unguided. You all landed in an ocean, but who can tell if it was the same one or at the same point of time? Also, there is a discrepancy in the time you thought you were gone and the actual time in this world. To us you seemed to be absent for a short time, but acccording to you a week or more had passed.' Luden sighed, regretful. 'I wish that it were possible to study the Jewel in detail. The instruments on the *Mordain* could tell us facts, but for now we can only speculate.'

In a generation or two, perhaps, it would be possible to subject the stone to scientific examination, but now that was impossible.

Kennedy looked up as Nava Sonega came toward them. He halted, his eyes enigmatic.

He said bluntly, 'Rem Naryan denies stealing the Jewel. He claims that you placed it within his quarters. Assuming this to be true, I wondered how it could have been done. Guards have investigated, and there is a passage that runs from your cham-

109

bers to those of the Chambodian delegation.'

Kennedy met his eyes. 'So?'

'There remains a doubt, my lord of Sergan, and one that must be resolved before the pact can be signed.'

'I don't understand,' said Luden acidly. 'Your warning to me was most explicit. If the Jewel was found, the one in possession would be impaled. Tradition, you said, demanded it. I fail to see your problem.'

'You animals!' From where he stood flanked by guards Rem Naryan lunged forward. 'You would condemn a civilized man to such a barbaric end? Is this Terran justice? To plant false evidence and make false accusations? I can prove that I did not steal the Jewel – can you?'

'I can!' Kennedy rose and met the vizier's eyes. 'Do you doubt that I am innocent?'

'You were gone!' stormed the Chambodian. Hate and fear had robbed him of self-control. 'Lying as good as dead. You had no right to return. I was sure that – ' He broke off, conscious of what he was saying.

'You were sure of what?' Kennedy's voice cracked like a whip, rising above the music, the sound of festival. It died as he sprang over the table, goblets crashing, wine spilling, cakes scattering from overturned dishes. 'Sure that I would die? As Hiton died? As Thom Ochran? And how could you be so sure – unless you engineered the whole thing?'

'I – '

'You deny it?' Kennedy stepped close to where the Chambodian stood. 'Do you deny that you want this world for the lamilite in the mountains? That you would turn this entire world into a mining camp and the people into slaves? That you've killed to get it and would kill again given the chance? Answer me, you swine!'

'My lord!' Rem Naryan turned to where Umed Khan sat, watching. 'I must protest. I am the representative of a powerful complex. I – '

'You are on Jarhen,' interrupted the ruler harshly. 'You will abide by our customs. Answer or be impaled!'

It had happened, Umed Khan thought grimly. Fate had provided the answer. The question of which power to join was about to be decided; not over the conference table, not even by the careful reading of omens, but by the actions of those involved. Plot and counterplot, intrigue and dissemination, lies

110

and truth, all now reduced to the area occupied by two men.

Nava Sonega said, his voice deep, 'You have heard the will of the Lord of Jarhen. Answer!'

'The creature lies!' Rem Naryan drew himself up to his full height. 'Monkey-men always lie. The animals don't know the meaning of truth.'

'You deny the accusation?'

'I ignore it!'

Kennedy stepped forward, catlike on his feet, both hands held a little before him, the palms stiff, fingers tight together. His voice was like iron.

'I challenge you, Chambodian. If you speak the truth, it will save you. If not, you will die.'

There was for Kennedy satisfaction in personal combat, in the use of his hands, in the sight of an enemy face. A face that had gloated over the deaths of Hiton and Ochran, and Kennedy's own peril. Rem Naryan belonged to a race that hated Earth and all it stood for, which would given the chance, turn worlds into dust in order to claim supremacy.

Luden said loudly, 'Cap!'

Unnoticed, he had charged the stone found on Hiton's body, holding the glowing jewel in the bowl of a spoon.

He said again, 'Cap! This will settle him!'

Instinctively the Chambodian turned, expecting to see a threat, a weapon aimed or ready to be thrown to a waiting hand. Instead he saw the glowing stone hurtling directly toward his eyes. For a moment he stared at it, concentrating on the missile. It was enough.

Luden activated the gem.

Kennedy turned as it pulsed, feeling his mind glow with familiar light, turning back in time to see Rem Naryan stagger, to fall twisting to the floor, water gushing from his open mouth.

Drowning as Hiton had drowned, as Thom Ochran, beneath the surface of an ocean aeons in the past.

MEWS BESTSELLERS

R 9   JOHN EAGLE 1: NEEDLES OF DEATH   *Paul Edwards*   40p

R 17   SATAN SLEUTH 1: FALLEN ANGEL   *Michael Avallone*   40p

R 25   SPIDER 1: DEATH REIGN OF THE VAMPIRE KING
     Grant Stockbridge   40p

R 92   SPIDER 2: HORDES OF THE RED BUTCHER
     Grant Stockbridge   40p

R 33   FATE 1: GALAXY OF THE LOST   *Gregory Kern*   40p

R106   FATE 2: SLAVESHIP FROM SERGAN   *Gregory Kern*   40p

R 41   JAMES GUNN 1: THE DEADLY STRANGER
     John Delaney   40p

R 68   CHURCHILL'S VIXENS 1: THE BRETON BUTCHER
     Leslie McManus   40p

R114   CHURCHILL'S VIXENS 2: THE BELGIAN FOX
     Leslie McManus   40p

R 76   THE BIG BRAIN 1: THE AARDVARK AFFAIR
     Gary Brandner   40p

R 84   THE CRAFT OF TERROR   *Ed. Peter Haining*   40p

R122   BLACK SCARAB   *Norman Gant*   40p

NEL P.O. BOX 11, FALMOUTH TR10 9EN, CORNWALL.

For U.K.: Customers should include to cover postage, 19p for the first book plus 9p per copy for each additional book ordered up to a maximum charge of 73p.

For B.F.P.O. and Eire: Customers should include to cover postage, 19p for the first book plus 9p per copy for the next 6 and thereafter 3p per book.

For Overseas: Customers should include to cover postage, 20p for the first book plus 10p per copy for each additional book.

Name ....

Address..

....

....

Title ....

Whilst every effort is made to maintain prices, new editions or printings may carry an increased price and the actual price of the edition supplied will apply.